The Salish Sea
Jewel of the Pacific Northwest

Audrey DeLella Benedict, *Cloud Ridge Naturalists* & Joseph K. Gaydos, *SeaDoc Society*

Printed in China using FSC papers

Published by Sasquatch Books

19 18 17 16 15   9 8 7 6 5 4 3 2 1

Published in collaboration with Cloud Ridge Publishing
and the SeaDoc Society
    Project manager: Wendy Shattil
    Editor: Alice Levine
    Book design: Ann W. Douden
    Photo editors: Wendy Shattil / Bob Rozinski
    Production: Betsy Armstrong
    Proofreader: Faith Marcovecchio

Book photographs: Contributing photographers listed on page 147
Front cover photograph: Top, Kevin Schafer; Bottom, Robin Lindsey
Back cover photograph: Drew Collins

Library of Congress Cataloging-in-Publication Data is available.

ISBN: 978-1-57061-985-4

Sasquatch Books
1904 Third Avenue, Suite 710
Seattle, WA 98101
(206) 467-4300
www.sasquatchbooks.com
custserv@sasquatchbooks.com

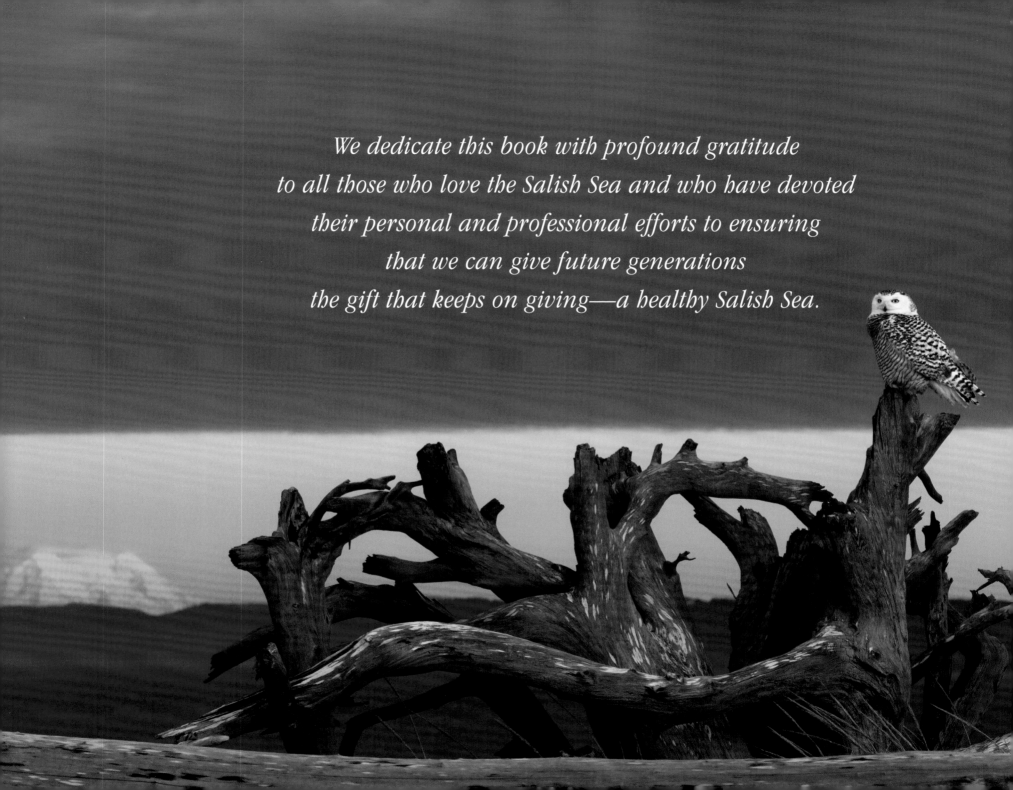

*We dedicate this book with profound gratitude
to all those who love the Salish Sea and who have devoted
their personal and professional efforts to ensuring
that we can give future generations
the gift that keeps on giving—a healthy Salish Sea.*

CONTENTS

The View from Raven's Roost   1

Voyages of discovery, ghost ships on the horizon, and the human history of the Salish Sea reveal the interwoven threads of the past and the present.

The Birth of a Sea   13

Beachcombing provides a portal to the geologic stories behind the scenery and the birth of an inland sea.

The Seafloor Revealed   29

Mirroring the Salish Sea's mountainous setting, the diversity of seafloor habitats and the tidal mixing of saltwater and freshwater in a life-nourishing alchemy result in unparalleled biological richness.

It Takes a Forest   39

The story behind the Salish Sea's remarkable biodiversity begins in the magnificent forests that cloak the seaward slopes of the Coast, Cascade, and Olympic Mountains.

Life at the Edges   51

Along the edges of the Salish Sea, the daily ebb and flood of the tides shape the rhythm of life and reveal fascinating unknown worlds.

Denizens of the Deep   65

The Salish Sea is home to an astonishing array of marine invertebrates ranging in size from microscopic species as exquisitely beautiful as snowflakes to some of the world's largest.

Bizarre and Beautiful Fish   75

In the cold-water world of the Salish Sea, the fish are as bizarre, as colorful, and as fascinating as any in the tropics.

Epic Journeys   85

Along the ancient pathways in the sky and in the waters of the Salish Sea, the annual migrations of birds and whales are awe-inspiring spectacles in the circle of life.

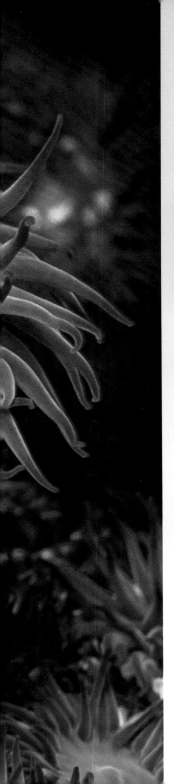

Aerial Acrobats and Deep Divers   95

Many of the Salish Sea's birds are amazing aerial acrobats, and others are as adept at "flying" underwater as they are soaring through the air.

Life in Two Worlds   105

Marine mammals possess an amazing ability to conduct most aspects of their lives underwater, even though they must breathe air.

Tidelines and Lifeways   117

We, as a critical part of the Salish Sea web of life, are acquiring the knowledge and skills to ensure a more resilient partnership between the land, the sea, and us.

Finding Hope in a Cautionary Tale   131

The Salish Sea offers a simple lesson: The more biologically diverse and healthy the sea is, the better it will adapt to change and the greater will be its ability to take care of us.

THE SALISH SEA

- Coastline length (including islands): 4,642 miles (7,470km)

- Total number of islands: 419, with a combined total land area of 1,413 square miles (3,660sq. km)

- Sea surface area: 6,535 square miles (16,925sq. km)

- Maximum depth: 2,133 feet (650m) at Bute Inlet, B.C.

- Human population: approximately 8 million

- Number of species: mammals, 38; birds, 172; fish, 253; reptiles, 2; and more than 3,000 macro-invertebrates (ones you can see without a microscope)

Campbell River, B.C.

STRAIT OF GEORGIA

VANCOUVER ISLAND

Vancouver, B.C.

Fraser River

Nanaimo, B.C.

GULF ISLANDS

Bellingham, WA

SAN JUAN ISLANDS

Skagit River

Port Renfrew, B.C.

Victoria, B.C.

Cape Flattery

STRAIT OF JUAN DE FUCA

N

PUGET SOUND

OLYMPIC PENINSULA

Seattle, WA

Olympia, WA

WHAT'S IN A NAME?

Bert Webber, a retired professor of environmental and marine science at Western Washington University and the driving force behind the naming of the Salish Sea, is quick to tell you that not having a name can create problems. In the early 1970s, people in Washington state were worried about the effect of oil tankers from Alaska passing through the Strait of Juan de Fuca to refinery facilities in the United States and Canada. The ensuing debate focused not only on the potential impact but also on what the region should be called. How does one address a possible problem when there isn't a name for the area where it might occur?

When a large-scale scientific study of the region showed the inland sea off the coast of Washington and British Columbia to be an integrated ecosystem that shares mixed saltwater and freshwater as well as similar marine life, it became clear that a single name for the sea was needed. In 1989, Webber requested that the Washington State Board on Geographic Names officially name the body of water consisting of the Puget Sound, the Strait of Juan de Fuca, and the Strait of Georgia, the Salish Sea. The board declined, stating that the name did not have popular usage. The first official recognition of the name came in 2008 by the Coast Salish, the region's original inhabitants and those the name is intended to honor. In 2009, the Washington State Board on Geographic Names, the U.S. Board on Geographic Names, the Geographical Names Board of Canada, and finally the Cabinet of the Province of British Columbia all approved Salish Sea as the name of this jewel of the Pacific Northwest.

I arise in the morning torn between the desire

to save the world and a desire to savor the world.

That makes it hard to plan the day.

—E. B. White

The View from Raven's Roost

Ocean and clouds conjoin—a quintessential Salish Sea morning. Imagine, for a moment, your view from a cliff-top aerie. The sea is the color of ancient jade. Rocky islets in the distance appear to float on luminous cushions of fog. The forest around you shimmers with raindrops, the air fragrant with the exhalations of Douglas fir and red cedar. A misty breeze riffles the water, carrying the evocative perfume of the sea at low tide. The raucous calls of black oystercatchers pierce the velvet quiet as they squabble over foraging rights to a newly emergent archipelago of tidepools. Suddenly, you hear a powerful whooshing sound and see a glistening black back and a tall dorsal fin—a male orca—cleave the smooth swell that lingers in the ropey fronds of kelp just off the point. Four more orcas surface in the male's wake, their smaller dorsal fins emerging in sequence as graceful as the opening of an oriental fan. Just as magically as they appeared, the five orcas blow in unison and then dive, disappearing into the depths. The clearing sky to the east reveals the snowy summit of Mount Baker rising above the fog like a ghost peak set adrift. There's no better place to be in the world at this moment.

1

◄ Mount Baker, called Komo Kulshan by the Coast Salish, rests quietly—for now. The volcano continues to release steam periodically from the Sherman Crater, and geologists predict a future eruption as explosive as that of Mount St. Helens in 1980.

Thousands of years before the first Europeans arrived in the Pacific Northwest, native peoples flourished along the shores of this magnificent inland sea. Named in honor of those first inhabitants and their modern descendants, the Salish Sea straddles the international border between Washington and British Columbia and includes the inland marine waters of the Strait of Juan de Fuca, Puget Sound, and the Strait of Georgia. Its waters embrace the southern end of Vancouver Island, the San Juan Islands, the Gulf Islands, and countless smaller islands. Oceanographers define it as an inland sea because it is largely landlocked, with the Strait of Juan de Fuca serving as the Salish Sea's primary portal to the Pacific Ocean. Tidal influence from the north, from Queen Charlotte Sound via Johnstone Strait and Discovery Passage, is minimal by comparison. The marine boundaries of the Salish Sea delineate all inland waters experiencing tidal exchange with the Pacific Ocean via the Strait of Juan de Fuca, creating an interconnected marine ecosystem that stretches from the south end of Washington's Puget Sound to British Columbia's Desolation Sound and the northernmost reaches of the Strait of Georgia. The Salish Sea is one of the world's largest inland seas, with a total marine area of about 7,000 square miles (18,130sq. km) and water depths in coastal fjords exceeding 2,000 feet (609m).

The Salish Sea is an ecological jewel—its remarkable biodiversity arising from the tide-swirled alchemy that occurs when land and sea are woven in an evolutionary fabric as old as time. This book conveys our sense of wonder and love for the Salish Sea and the life it sustains in a seascape of deep fjords, rocky islands, sheltered bays and inlets, and verdant estuaries nourished by vast networks of braided rivers. We also acknowledge what is at risk for the Salish Sea if we continue to unravel the intricate threads that bind these precious ecosystems before we have even begun to fully understand their complexities. Profound changes have occurred in the ecological health of the Salish Sea and its surrounding watersheds in the geologic blink of an eye. Nearly 8 million people live and work along the coast and in the mainland watersheds of the Salish Sea or on one of its many islands—their livelihoods, economic well-being, and quality of life depend on how we shape its future. We've lost much, and we risk far more if we fail to remember that the Salish Sea links us to the vast global ocean. This book is a visual celebration, not a requiem—laced throughout with heart and hope because citizens and scientists are working side by side as ocean stewards toward a vision of sustainability in a changing world.

Divers might think the extraordinarily diverse and spectacular marine life of painted and pink-tipped anemones and red soft corals had been magically transported from a tropical coral reef to the Pacific Northwest.

A humpback whale works a food-rich tidal current where schools of small forage fish, probably herring, have formed a sparkling spherical mass to evade predation. Between the whale, the circling rhinoceros auklets, and the opportunistic gulls, this fish buffet is well attended.

A floral display on Yellow Island rivals the color palette of the seafloor and often includes succulents, such as broad-leaved yellow stonecrop and brittle prickly pear cactus, and a dazzle of paintbrushes, chocolate lilies, and blue camas.

VOYAGES OF DISCOVERY

Fog-shrouded days at sea remind us of the ancient mariners who traveled these waters without benefit of electronic charts, radar, or other modern navigational aids. Voyages of discovery have illuminated the spirit and captured the imagination of adventurers throughout history. The place-names we see on modern maps of the Salish Sea reflect hundreds of centuries of human interactions with both land and sea—a multilingual, cartographic narrative of Pacific maritime history. We tend to romanticize Europe's Age of Discovery, forgetting that the first European mariners to explore the Salish Sea were sailing into waters known to indigenous people for thousands of years. Coast Salish oral cartography—names handed down from one generation to another—identifies places having geographic, spiritual, or tribal group significance. These names reflect the bounty of land and sea—the great gifts, or *S'abadeb,* in the Salish language. The lifeways and cultures that evolved along the shores of the Salish Sea are a celebration of ingenuity and brilliant adaptation to an ever-changing environment.

Salmon have always been the spirit food of the Coast Salish. The names given to major river watersheds, such as the Cowichan, Duwamish, Elwha, Nisqually, Nooksack, and Skokomish, delineate each tribal group's homeland and rightful claim to specific salmon spawning waters. In each case, the entire watershed was crucial to the annual life cycle of salmon as well as to the people who depended on the fish for their survival. In late summer and fall, thousands of spawning salmon filled these streams and rivers—shimmering streaks of silver, green, and red swimming upstream to their natal waters. At the end of the spawning season, with the scent of ghost salmon still lingering in the air, the coastal fishing camps were abandoned and people returned to the winter villages within the sheltering embrace of the forest—a watershed transhumance unlike any on Earth.

◄ This photograph from 1915 shows the Makah at Cape Flattery, near the mouth of the Strait of Juan de Fuca, bringing a halibut catch to the beach where the women can cut the fish for drying and storage. Edward Sheriff Curtis (1868–1952), widely accepted as the early photographer most respected by First Nations peoples, did not intend to document primitivism but to portray the cultural beauty and lifeways of people he admired and respected. When he embarked on his 30-year project to document the lives of Native American peoples before the onslaught of irreversible change, photography was in its infancy. Curtis was never to realize the impact his photographic legacy and 6,000-plus pages of ethnographic detail would have on future generations.

Pink salmon arrive at the mouth of their spawning river.

GHOST SHIPS ON THE HORIZON

Sleeping volcanoes still watch over the entrance to the Strait of Juan de Fuca—just as they did when the strait's namesake paced the deck of his caravel in 1592. Mapmakers had long speculated that a Northwest Passage—Marco Polo's Strait of Anian—must surely exist across the top of the world. Juan de Fuca's orders from the Spanish crown were explicit—finish the charting of the Pacific coastline north of Mexico and locate, once and for all, the ever-elusive Strait of Anian. The Greek-born pilot and mariner had already succeeded in sailing farther north along the Pacific coast of North America than any European before him. Having been bedeviled offshore for days by an impenetrable wall of coastal fog, Juan de Fuca must have felt the looming specter of defeat hovering at his shoulder as he stood watch at the helm. His lateen-rigged caravel was the fastest and best sailing vessel of its day, with a unique sail design that allowed it to head into the wind and a shallow keel that made it highly maneuverable in coastal waters.

Waves thunder against the rocks at the mouth of the Strait of Juan de Fuca near Port Renfrew (B.C.). On the Washington side of the strait, many believe the high pinnacle of rock (above), noted by de Fuca in his logbook, to be modern-day Fuca Pillar, one of the most dramatic of the sea stacks near the tip of Cape Flattery. From 1830 to 1925, the time of sailing ships, 137 major sea disasters occurred near the entrance to the strait, prompting mariners to nickname it Graveyard of the Pacific. Today, this marine wilderness is an integral part of the Olympic Coast National Marine Sanctuary, which measures 2,408 square nautical miles (8,270sq. km).

Imagine the shouts of jubilation from the weary men as strong easterly winds began to build, billowing the caravel's sails and dissipating the fog that had obscured the coast. Did the wind carry the smell of land—the sweet fragrance of cedar, wet ferns, and salal? What the men saw was a broad and dangerously beautiful portal guarded by great pillars of rock. It was clear that the Pacific flowed eastward into the unknown interior of the continent—a siren call that could not be ignored. According to the ship's log, the caravel sailed past a prominent rock (now called Fuca Pillar) and into a "broad Inlet of the Sea, betweene 47 and 48 degrees Latitude." Believing he'd found the Strait of Anian and the passage to the North Sea, Juan de Fuca explored these sheltered waters for twenty days, reporting to his Spanish employers that he'd sailed this broad inlet of the sea in its entirety, the tides carrying his ship north through a chain of "divers islands," past encampments "with natives clad in skins of beastes." The Spanish dismissed his discovery, and no record of it exists in Spain's maritime archives. Had it not been for a meeting in 1596 between the aging mariner and Michael Lok, the English consul to Venice, we might never have known that Juan de Fuca existed—or what he discovered. The bitter struggle between Spain and England for control of the North Pacific would last for nearly two centuries before the "rediscovery" of Juan de Fuca's legendary waterway by British Captain Charles Barkley in 1787 set the stage for another great mariner, Captain George Vancouver.

◄ Sunset casts an amber glow across the Strait of Georgia to distant Vancouver Island as cloud-like flocks of migrating seabirds fly north over the Salish Sea.

Vancouver's expedition has been called the greatest marine survey of all time. Not only was Vancouver charged with conducting a survey of the coastline of western North America, he was ordered to make a full reconnaissance of the Strait of Juan de Fuca, the Strait of Georgia, and the waters leading to the north end of Vancouver Island. Under Vancouver's command were two extremely seaworthy vessels: the 100-foot (30m) three-masted sloop of war *Discovery* and the 53-foot (16m) brig *Chatham*, with Lieutenant William Broughton at the helm. The expedition included Archibald Menzies, the surgeon-naturalist, whose detailed descriptions of the flora and fauna are immortalized in many of the scientific names we use today. Other key members of the expedition included Peter Puget, Joseph Baker, Joseph Whidbey, and James Johnstone—their names and those of many more are inscribed in bold on maps of the Salish Sea.

Dungeness Spit—a slender 4-mile (6.4km) ridge of log-strewn sand—curves eastward into the Strait of Juan de Fuca as if beckoning seafarers to seek respite in the shallow bay behind the spit. Seabirds and shorebirds know these sheltered waters well, gathering by the thousands each winter and early spring to ride out the fierce storms that batter the coast. When Vancouver's ships anchored there on May Day in 1792, the safe moorage would have been a welcome respite and spring migration would have been at its peak. Far to the east, a snow-capped volcano rose above the clouds like a sentinel; Vancouver named it Mount Baker (called Komo Kulshan by the Coast Salish) after his trusty lieutenant, Joseph Baker. To the southeast, yet another majestic volcano (called Tahoma by the Coast Salish) would be named Mount Rainier. As Vancouver and Broughton would later discover when they encountered two Spanish *goletas* under the command of Alcalá Galiano and Cayetano Valdés, the Spanish also had extensive knowledge of the geography of the region, had already explored several straits, and had named the San Juan Islands and several of the Gulf Islands.

Vancouver had seen much of the world from the deck of a ship and was seldom given to hyperbole, yet he pronounced all they beheld to be "enchantingly beautiful . . . the country before us exhibited everything that bounteous nature could be expected to draw into one point of view." His journals also provided our first glimpse of the Coast Salish people and a lifeway honed by centuries of experience in harvesting and preserving the bounty of the sea and the land.

The publication of Vancouver's charts and journals put the Pacific Northwest on the world map. Nothing would ever be the same. Vancouver's glowing descriptions of all aspects of the Salish Sea, the scenery, the deep and sheltered bays, the immense trees, the abundant natural resources, and the friendliness of the native people amounted to an irresistible invitation to colonize. Imagine standing alongside Juan de Fuca today, sailing along this extraordinary waterway and seeing through his eyes the changes wrought over the course of four centuries. What would he think about the future of the Salish Sea?

Nearly 8 million people live and work along the coast and in the mainland watersheds of the Salish Sea, or on one of its many islands. Their livelihoods, economic well-being, and quality of life depend on how we shape the future of this magnificent landscape.

11

Rock carries its own epithets,
its own refrains.
—John McPhee

The Birth of a Sea

Almost no one can resist picking up a wave-polished stone and admiring its colors and pattern. Beachcombing can be both a meditation and a portal to the past. The stones at our feet are richly illustrated texts, telling gothic tales of cataclysmic fires deep within the Earth, the breakup of ancient continents, the birth of oceans, erupting volcanoes, surging rivers of glacial ice, and the reincarnation of new landscapes from old. Countless stories are encapsulated in each stone, and many of these stories describe geologic events beyond imagination. The colossal changes that occurred as the ancestral North American continent expanded westward—shape-shifting on a grand scale—can be read in the extraordinary diversity of rock types we find today along the shores of the Salish Sea. Think of these stones as chapters in an autobiography—a rich and marvelously idiosyncratic geologic history unlike any other.

Each stone on the beach at Washington's Birch Bay State Park represents a chapter in the geologic story of the Salish Sea and its surrounding mountains. Igneous, metamorphic, and sedimentary rock origins are all represented here, and the vibrant colors you see reflect the various minerals in each stone. For most of these surf-polished stones, this beach is just the latest stop on a journey that began millions of years ago.

Deep within Olympic National Park, the Elwha River rushes through Goblin Gates on its way to the Strait of Juan de Fuca.

This sea of peaks in the North Cascades is typical of the crystalline rocks that originated deep within the Earth's crust and then were uplifted millions of years later to face the ravages of erosion at the Earth's surface. The spectacular scenery we see today reflects the profound artistry of rushing waters and rivers of glacial ice over the past 2 million years.

READING THE ROCKS

The Pacific Northwest is one of the youngest and most geologically dynamic places on Earth. The volcanoes and mountain landscapes that frame the shores of today's Salish Sea were born in the regional epicenter of the Ring of Fire—the geologically active zone that rims the Pacific Ocean. The volcanic and seismic activity associated with this zone is the result of plate tectonics—a deep-earth process powered by immense geothermal convection currents. The planet's rigid surface is broken into 10 large oceanic and continental crustal plates and several microplates that are moving relative to each other and at different speeds over the underlying molten mantle. Without plate tectonics, there would be no ocean basins, islands, continents, mountains, volcanoes, and no Salish Sea.

Imagine the Earth's plates as a restless jigsaw puzzle of slip-sliding, diverging, and colliding crustal slabs. Where plates slip past each other horizontally along a fault or fracture system, frictional drag triggers stress-relieving earthquakes. Where plates diverge, ocean basins are created and basaltic magma rises from the mantle to fill the void along the divergent boundary and create new oceanic crust. When an oceanic and a continental plate collide, the heavier iron-rich oceanic crust plunges beneath the lighter silica-rich continental crust by a process called subduction.

The subduction zone serves as the crucible in which descending oceanic slabs undergo the ultimate geologic recycling—melting, dehydration, recrystallization, and eventual rebirth as new crust added to the overriding plate. Reading the evidence in the rocks, scientists are deciphering—episode by episode—the geologic and biological evolution of the Salish Sea.

THE SALISH SEA STORY BEGINS

About 220 million years ago, the ancestral North American continent was part of supercontinent Pangaea, a single landmass surrounded by Earth's only ocean. With the break-up of Pangaea, tectonic events sent the North American Plate moving westward on a collision course with the Pacific Plate—a process that continues today. In the first act of the geologic evolution of the Pacific Northwest, the western shoreline of the ancestral North American continent was approximately where the Rocky Mountains are today. Over the next 200 million years, more than 400 miles (644km) of new land would be added to the northwestern edge of the North American Plate; today that land encompasses most of present-day Washington, British Columbia, and Alaska.

With the retreat of Ice Age glaciers, wind and wave action transformed Sucia's shoreline, creating wave-cut platforms and reefs, exposing layers of fossil-bearing rocks, sculpting the sandstone into fanciful shapes, and salt-etching sandstone rocks with a distinctive honeycomb weathering pattern.

◄ In the San Juan Islands, Sucia and Patos Islands are among the region's most beautiful geologic playgrounds. Canadian Gulf Islands, such as Hornby and Gabriola, offer similar geologic opportunities for exploration. As this aerial view portrays, these accreted island arcs consist of folded and uplifted sedimentary rock layers derived from seafloor- or river-transported sediments. Differential erosion of the more resistant sandstone and conglomerate layers creates the horseshoe-shaped ridges we see today.

The spectacular geologic setting of the Salish Sea was created by two types of violent subduction at plate margins. When two plates carrying oceanic crust collide, the process of subduction builds an offshore arc-shaped chain of volcanic islands called an island arc. A continental arc forms when an oceanic plate plunges beneath the continental margin, which triggers volcanoes at the surface and the massive intrusion of silica-rich magma at greater depth. This collision-driven "docking" of island arcs and seafloor sediments along the continental margin was anything but gentle—more of a shipwreck of contorted upthrust rock. Geologists describe the setting of the Salish Sea as a complex mosaic of continental and island arcs. The extraordinary diversity of rock types on our beaches transports us back in time to distant mountain ranges and to the bottom of ancient seas.

The high peaks and alpine uplands of the North Cascades are formed of a complex assortment of crystalline rocks that originated deep within the Earth's crust and rose along the continental margin in a relatively recent series of colossal uplifts. Erosion's handiwork presents a dramatic backdrop for the Salish Sea.

A CRETACEOUS SEA BOTH STRANGE AND FAMILIAR

Ammonites, shelled cephalopod relatives of octopus and squid, swam in Cretaceous seas and represent the climax of mollusk evolution. Exquisitely beautiful ammonite fossils—a Sucia Island specialty—can be the size of a dinner plate. With shells ranging in size from less than an inch (2.5cm) to more than 12 feet (3.6m) across, these remarkable animals had gas-filled chambers in their shells that provided essential buoyancy. Ammonites were the first swimming carnivores in the oceans and remained among the dominant marine predators for nearly 300 million years. More than 10,000 fossil ammonite species have been found around the world, their shell shapes varying from straight to coiled to elaborate candy cane–striped contraptions known for their structural beauty. All ammonites disappeared from the Late Cretaceous seas 65 million years ago, one among many extinction casualties associated with the explosive impact of the Chicxulub comet off Mexico's Yucatán Peninsula. Giant marine reptiles and thousands of other life-forms shared the fate of the ammonites in the Late Cretaceous.

Imagine taking a time-machine dive in the Cretaceous-age Salish Sea and catching a glimpse of a mosasaur or a plesiosaur, giant marine reptiles thought to be the most ferocious predators in the Mesozoic seas. Our craft would be dwarfed by the gigantic skull of the mosasaur discovered on Hornby Island or the perfectly fossilized 50-foot (15.2m) skeleton of a seagoing plesiosaur recovered on Vancouver Island. Many species of ammonites and nautiloids swim past, gracefully propelled by their circular array of long tentacles. At depths of 100 feet (30.4m) or more, the ammonites search the muddy seafloor for worms, snails, clams, oysters, sea urchins, and crustaceans. Some of the clams and snails look like those in the modern Salish Sea, while many others resemble ones we would expect to see in shallow tropical seas of the coral reef latitudes. Passing over a bubbly area on the seafloor, we see a dense community of inoceramid clams, much like the hubcap-sized fossils found at Hornby and a few other islands. These clams are believed to have clustered around hydrothermal vents and were adapted to a diet of methane-loving bacteria rather than plankton.

A song sparrow enjoys a beachside view atop a cairn of granite cobbles.

One of many deep glacially striated grooves in the summit bedrock of Cypress Island.

Ice-transported boulders, called glacial erratics, at Iceberg Point on Lopez Island.

The mountain ranges that embrace the Salish Sea are dynamic systems in the still-unfolding story. The tectonic forces of volcanism, mountain building, and regional uplift that created Vancouver Island's Insular Mountains and the Coast, Cascade, and Olympic Ranges are forever keeping pace with surface weathering and erosion processes. As mountains in tectonically active regions erode, uplift occurs as hotter and deeper crustal rock moves toward the surface in areas where erosion rates are greatest. In the mountains surrounding the Salish Sea, higher elevation resulted in more precipitation, mountain glaciation, and ever-deeper incisement of rivers and streams—three of the most powerful erosion tools on Earth.

Water in all its forms—mist, rain, snow, ice, and glacial meltwater—serves gravity extremely well in sculpting landscapes. In fact, uplifts and their associated fault systems established the flow direction and drainage patterns of the modern river systems that nourish the Salish Sea. The Fraser River, regarded by some as the Salish Sea's most critical source of freshwater, reversed its direction entirely from a northward- to a southward-draining watershed system emptying into the Strait of Georgia—just one example of the many profound linkages between geology and biology that shape our world.

Hikers standing atop the 2,297-foot (700m) summit of The Chief in British Columbia's Stawamus Chief Provincial Park are rewarded with a spectacular view of Howe Sound. This massive granodiorite dome, called a pluton, is one of many such granitic intrusions that make up the Coast Mountains, which are considered in their entire extent to be the single largest contiguous granite outcropping in the world. The Chief's steep glacially polished walls and the glacial striations on its summit indicate that the entire mountain was covered in ice and shaped by glacial erosion.

From the summit of Mount Baker, a fiery sunset spreads across the islands of the Salish Sea.

What we see today—the Salish Sea and its ice-sculpted backdrop—is largely the creation of the most recent Pleistocene glacial episode, the Fraser Glaciation. The saga began with the formation of a major ice sheet in the Canadian Cordillera between 30,000 and 25,000 years ago, concurrent with the last major advances of valley glaciers from the Coast Mountains, the Cascades, and the Olympics. The Cordilleran Ice Sheet spread south across today's international border 20,000 years ago, filling the ancestral Strait of Georgia and merging with glaciers flowing out of Vancouver Island's mountains and from the Coast Mountains, the Fraser Valley, and the Cascades. By 17,000 years ago, mainland valley glaciers had already begun to retreat in response to a warming climate. The Cordilleran Ice Sheet, powered by its sheer mass, continued advancing for several thousand more years, smothering the southeastern end of Vancouver Island, the Gulf Islands, and the San Juan archipelago in a stupendous blanket of ice. The Fraser Glaciation, which marked the final advance of the Cordilleran Ice Sheet, reached the north end of the Olympic Peninsula about 16,000 years ago, damming the Puget Basin with a wall of ice 60 miles (96.6km) wide.

The Puget Sound and Juan de Fuca Lobes of the Fraser Glaciation reached their maximum extent about 14,000 years ago, with the Puget Lobe pushing as far south as modern-day Tenino in the Puget Lowland, and the Juan de Fuca Lobe spreading west to meet the Pacific Ocean. During the glacial maximum, the Cordilleran Ice Sheet would have been nearly 8,000 feet (1.8km) thick above present-day Vancouver, at least 6,000 feet (2km) deep over Bellingham, and more than 3,000 feet (1km) thick above Seattle.

By 13,500 years ago, the shift to a warmer climate caused the ice lobes to retreat rapidly, generating huge volumes of meltwater. The seafloor effects of all this water can be seen in the drainage channels now occupied by Lake Sammamish, Lake Washington, Puget Sound, and the Hood Canal. With the ice sheet in retreat mode, the Pacific Ocean flowed into the Strait of Juan de Fuca. By 10,000 years ago, the Strait of Georgia was also completely ice free. The three fjords—the Strait of Juan de Fuca, Puget Sound, and the Strait of Georgia—now formed an interconnected inland waterway dotted with islands both large and small. The Salish Sea was born anew, with a glacial imprint that would determine its future as one of the world's most biologically rich inland seas.

◀ The combined effects of glacial abrasion and plucking can be seen in the streamlined bedrock landforms called whalebacks, which are commonly observed on the floors of glaciated valleys. If it were possible to peel away the blanket of vegetation on many of the islands in the Salish Sea, their distinctive shape and profile would be revealed. The abrasion-smoothed right end of this whaleback indicates the direction the glacier came from, and the steep glacially-plucked left side is the direction the glacier was headed. This glacial whaleback, like others, provides a perfect haul out for Steller sea lions.

Sunset view looking west toward Howe Sound from the seaside village of Horseshoe Bay, which is located on Vancouver's North Shore and serves as a gateway for the British Columbia ferry to central Vancouver Island. Horseshoe Bay is also the starting point of the scenic Sea-to-Sky Highway (Highway 93), which winds through the Coast Mountains and Garibaldi Provincial Park.

When I think of the floor of the deep sea, . . .
I always see the steady, unremitting, downward drift
of materials from above, flake upon flake, layer upon layer—
a drift that has continued for hundreds of millions of years,
that will go as long as there are seas and continents.

—Rachel Carson

The Seafloor Revealed

Sit quietly and listen to the sea's rhythmic chanting and soft percussion. The fluid crescendo of waves exploding against the rocks, the rainstick sound of beach pebbles shifting back and forth with the incoming tide, and the deep basso exultation as the tidal surge retreats are among the most hypnotic sounds on Earth. Imagine the complex worlds that lie beneath the midnight blue opacity of the Salish Sea. A scuba diver would see marine life as exuberantly colored as a field of wildflowers—orange sea pens, white plumose anemones, red sea urchins, candy stripe shrimp, purple sea stars, and copper-hued rockfish. Using multibeam sonar and airborne laser (lidar) technology, submersibles, and underwater video cameras, scientists are now able to map the complex topography of the seafloor and its dazzling array of marine habitats. This quintessential *geodiversity*, a new word in our scientific lexicon, sets the stage for the diverse habitats that create the Salish Sea's biological richness.

UNDERSEA HABITATS

Boldly mirroring the Salish Sea's mountainous setting, bathymetric mapping of the seafloor reveals the interplay of plate tectonics and the culminating sculptural magic wrought by thousands of feet of glacial ice. Water depths in the Salish Sea are highly variable as a result of these incredible geologic processes. Wherever glaciers carved a path through the mountains, near-vertical fjord walls are juxtaposed against deep water close to shore. Almost anywhere along one of these fjords, a child could throw a rock from shore and have it tumble to a depth of 200 feet (60m) or more. In North America's other great estuary, the Chesapeake Bay, where the average depth is 21 feet (6.5m), one would be hard-pressed to find a place in the middle of the bay where the depth is even 175 feet (52m).

The geodiversity of the seafloor offers an array of distinctive habitats for marine life adapted to the unique living conditions that occur in each type. Underwater evidence of glaciation can be seen in the form of striated bedrock, ice-grooved troughs, U-shaped submarine valleys, cross-channel sills, moraine-dammed embayments, and fluted banks of sediment. Glaciers delivered massive quantities of rock, gravel, sand, and mud to Puget Sound, the Strait of Georgia, and the Strait of Juan de Fuca, depositing these sediments wherever geologic obstructions slowed the flow of ice or when glaciers "paused" as they advanced or retreated. Wavelike deposits of sand—submerged dune fields—reflect the underwater artistry of tidal currents. Bathymetric maps also identify tectonically active areas on the seafloor—fault traces, earthquake-generated rock slides, and the gas-emitting pockmarks

Widespread and variably colored, this aggregation of painted anemones lives in the midst of an equally colorful array of sponges.

(seafloor craters) associated with fault zones—a reminder that the Juan de Fuca Plate remains a vital force in the Salish Sea.

Tidepooling in the intertidal zone—the narrow band of shoreline between high and low tides—offers a fascinating window into the nearshore marine world. Unless you are a diver, the opportunity to observe marine life in deeper waters is rare. Each marine habitat type harbors a distinctive community of plants and animals evolutionarily adapted to the physical and biological challenges posed by their environment. Submerged mountains with ledges and jumbles of loose rock are common in the Salish Sea, providing critical living space for

Of the reef-forming glass sponges, the cloud sponge is the only species that produces cloud-like growths. These growths provide shelter for an amazing array of wildlife, such as the juvenile rockfish shown, and seem to function as a mini-ecosystem.

numerous species of rockfish, northern abalone, and many other iconic species. Glass sponge reefs are a unique habitat type that requires low-relief glacial sediment banks on which to establish. These ancient reefs, which may reach heights of 50 feet (15m) or more, offer a silica-filigreed refuge for juvenile rockfish and other small marine animals. Easily damaged by human activities because of their glass-like fragility, sponge reefs are exceedingly rare and under consideration for marine-protected status.

Marine animals preferring fine-textured sediments on the seafloor, either for protective

The starry flounder, which can be right eyed or left eyed, rests partially or completely submerged in soft substrates at depths as shallow as the intertidal zone. This perfectly camouflaged fish can sometimes be seen undulating along the bottom in search of prey in areas adjacent to eelgrass beds and even in the brackish waters near the mouths of rivers.

Kevin Campion, captain of the Seattle-based Deep Green Wilderness vessel, the S/V *Orion*, sails with his crew along the Fraser River sediment plume.

◀ The dendritic artistry of flow channels traverses a sandy mudflat near Fidalgo Bay and Padilla Bay.

camouflage, burrowing, or filter-feeding lifestyles, have myriad choices. Underwater dune fields offer the perfect escape cover for Pacific sand lance, a vital forage fish for marine mammals, salmon, and diving seabirds. To evade these skillful predators, the masterful sand lance burrows face-first into sand or fine gravel.

Wherever rivers and streams empty into sheltered bays, fine sediments have accumulated in the form of subtidal deltas and mudflats, providing ideal living conditions for filter-feeding shellfish and other invertebrates as well as foraging areas for migratory and resident bird species that depend on these species for food. In fact, the abundance of these soft sediment-rich habitats, nutrient-rich water, and the unusually broad intertidal zone supports world-class conditions for shellfish. As marine geologist Gary Greene says, "Geology controls everything." The Salish Sea's quintessential geodiversity and the important role that seafloor topography plays in mixing nutrient-rich seawater and freshwater sets the stage for the inland sea's extraordinary biological productivity.

HOW THE SALISH SEA WORKS

Estuaries—where rivers flow into the sea—are magical places: the tug of the moon powers the tidal mixing of saltwater and freshwater in a life-nourishing alchemy. The Salish Sea is an estuary unlike any other. Tidal currents—two ebb and two flood tides each day—drive the inland sea's circulation engine. The Strait of Juan de Fuca is the principal waterway connecting the marine basins of the Strait of Georgia and the Puget Sound with the Pacific Ocean. Throughout the Salish Sea, water depths are highly variable, with maximum localized depths ranging from 2,132 feet (650m) in the coastal fjords to depths of 400 to 700 feet (122 to 213m) in the waters surrounding the San Juan and Gulf Islands—a reflection of the profound geodiversity of the seafloor.

33

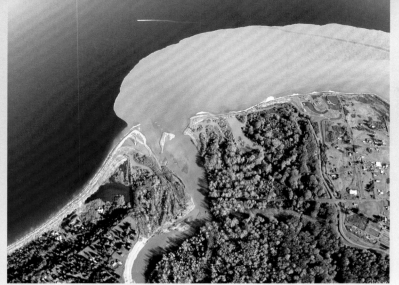

More than 20 years after the U.S. Congress passed the Elwha Ecosystem and Fisheries Restoration Act in 1992, the largest dam removal project in the world was completed. The dismantling of the Elwha Dam and the Glines Canyon Dam, an environmental triumph, opened 70 miles of spawning habitat to steelhead and all 5 species of Pacific salmon. With the rebirth of the Elwha River in March 2012, a century's worth of dam-blocked sediment fanned out at the river's mouth into the Strait of Juan de Fuca.

◄ THE MIGHTY FRASER RIVER

Of all the rivers and streams that discharge freshwater into the Salish Sea, the Fraser River, shown depositing its milky-green sediment-laden water into the Strait of Georgia, is by far the largest contributor. At the river's peak in the late summer, thanks to the melted remains of once mountaintop snow, the mighty Fraser can pump 2.6 million gallons of water a second (10,000m³/s) into the Salish Sea. During this summer freshet, the Fraser's magnificent plume forms a surface layer 6 to 33 feet (2 to 10m) thick that can be seen jetting across to the Gulf Islands (as in this image). Alternately, if the prevailing wind is from the northwest, the plume might blanket the southern Strait of Georgia. Or if there is a strong enough flood tide without much wind, the plume can be carried into the northern Strait of Georgia.

The vital river arteries that nourish the Salish Sea with freshwater—the Fraser, Nooksack, Skagit, Snohomish, Duwamish, Puyallup, and Nisqually, and on the Olympic Peninsula, the Skokomish, Quilcene, Dungeness, and Elwha—are born amid majestic glacier-riven peaks and old-growth forests. Together, the Pacific Ocean and the mountain ranges that tower above the Salish Sea profoundly influence the regional climate. As moisture-laden air from the Pacific flows eastward and ascends the steep west-facing slopes of the Coast, Cascade, and Olympic Mountains, the air cools, and windward slopes capture the majority of the moisture as fog, rain, and snow. The Pacific Northwest's infamous wet season, which accounts for 75 percent of the region's annual precipitation, generally begins in October, peaks in midwinter, and winds down by April. Although the western slopes of the mountains receive enormous quantities of snow and rain, often exceeding 200 inches (508cm) of moisture a year, other locations, such as Sequim and the San Juan Islands, lie in the rain shadow of the Olympic Mountains and average 32 inches (81cm) a year. The magnificent coniferous forests that cloak the windward slopes of the region's mountains and the watersheds they nourish are a gift of this beneficence. More than 70 percent of the total freshwater inflow for the entire Salish Sea comes from British Columbia's Fraser River watershed.

Rivers deliver an abundance of nutrients, sediment, and other organic materials to the Salish Sea. This freshwater contribution to the estuarine system varies seasonally and interannually. Estuarine currents are superimposed on daily tides and are driven by the hydraulic head of the Fraser River as it enters the Strait of Georgia near Vancouver. Because freshwater is less dense than saltwater, for most of the year the Salish Sea experiences a net seaward outflow of less salty water at the surface toward the Strait of Juan de Fuca from all mainland watersheds and a net inflow of Pacific Ocean water at depth. Water quality and chemistry reflect ocean conditions, storm systems, and prevailing winds. Wintertime gales, with storm system

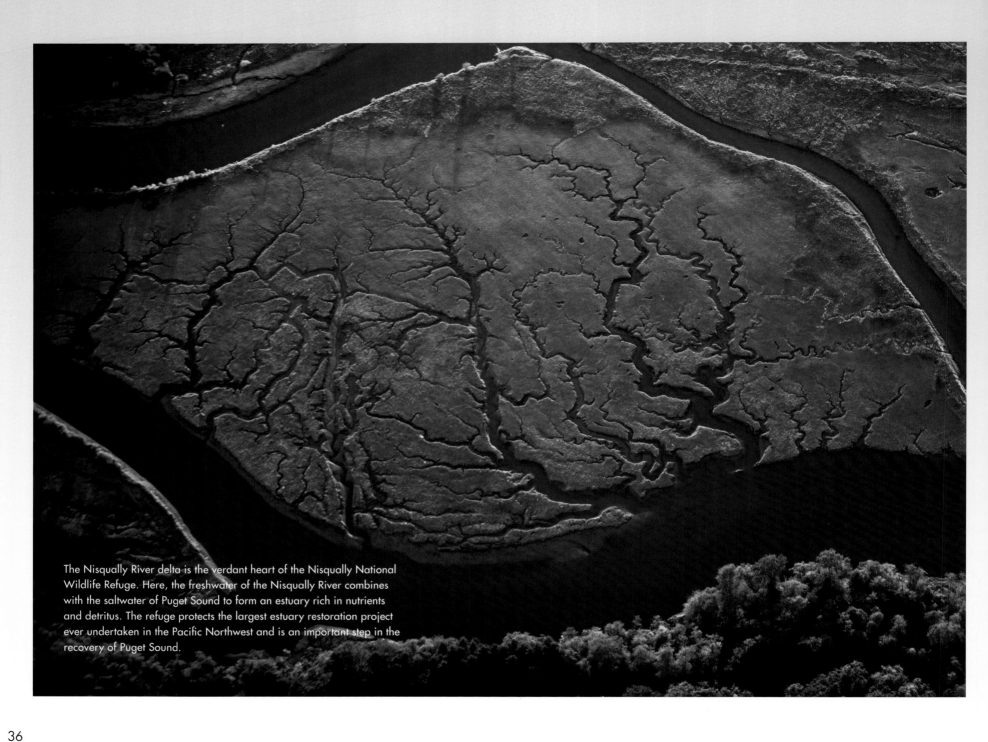

The Nisqually River delta is the verdant heart of the Nisqually National Wildlife Refuge. Here, the freshwater of the Nisqually River combines with the saltwater of Puget Sound to form an estuary rich in nutrients and detritus. The refuge protects the largest estuary restoration project ever undertaken in the Pacific Northwest and is an important step in the recovery of Puget Sound.

wind speeds ranging between 40 and 80 miles per hour (64 to 128kph), are not uncommon in the Strait of Juan de Fuca and the Strait of Georgia. Winds predominantly from the north tend to push water off the coasts of Washington and British Columbia at the surface, causing an upwelling of water that is nutrient-rich but low in oxygen. Strong winds from the south push water onto the coastal shelf, causing a downwelling of water that is nutrient-poor but rich in oxygen.

Salish Sea tidal currents are influenced by seasonal storm systems, by shifts in wind speed and direction, and by underwater sills or other geologic obstructions. Marine scientist Terrie Klinger describes the mountains along the seafloor of the San Juan Islands as the "egg beater" of the Salish Sea because of their important role in mixing outflowing estuarine surface water with incoming nutrient-rich ocean water. Tidal exchanges forced through relatively shallow or narrow reaches can routinely generate currents up to 9 knots (16.7kph), such as those seen at Deception Pass or at Admiralty Inlet, or can even exceed 16 knots (29.6kph) at places like Skookumchuck Narrows at the entrance of Sechelt Inlet in British Columbia. As tidal currents flow past points of land, the water swirls in eddies in the lee of the point, bringing nutrients and plankton to nearshore marine communities. The exchange of water, sediment, and nutrients between the land and the sea is fundamental to the formation and maintenance of a rich array of marine habitats.

The Skagit River and its tributaries drain an area of 1.7 million acres (6,900sq. km) in the Cascade Range of the state of Washington and British Columbia before emptying into the Salish Sea. It is the only large river system in Washington that contains healthy populations of all 5 native salmon species and 3 anadromous trout species. The Skagit River estuary also supports the largest wintering concentration of bald eagles in the continental United States. Fertile agricultural fields now dominate the Skagit's lower reaches.

Douglas fir is the most common conifer in coastal forests. This beautiful evergreen is a pioneer species, intolerant of shade, and will thrive for hundreds of years until it is overtopped by shade-loving species, such as western red cedar or western hemlock.

When we try to pick out anything by itself,
we find it hitched to everything else
in the universe. —John Muir

It Takes a Forest

Standing in a grove of ancient trees, we are reminded of a Coast Salish story from the beginning of time when Raven slipped from the shadow of a giant cedar to steal sunlight and cast the moon and stars into the heavens. Beneath an arching canopy of soaring red cedars and western hemlocks, the floor of Raven's forest is carpeted with emerald-green moss and decorated with sword fern, blueberry, and salal. Even the air is pungently organic—the forest alive, breathing, and wet with promise. The ethereal flutelike song of a Swainson's thrush pours down from a high ridge. Other voices join the streamside harmonic: the high sweet notes of a golden kinglet, the haunting whistle of a varied thrush, and the bravado trill of a Pacific wren. A small gray bird—an American dipper—launches from a boulder in midstream and plunges fearlessly into the swift current to search for aquatic delicacies on the streambed. Emerging triumphant, droplets of water sparkling like diamonds on its wings, the dipper holds a salmon egg in its beak. If we followed the dipper on its upstream journey, we would simply be tracing one strand of life through this extraordinarily interconnected ecosystem. In the purest sense, Raven's forest is a single towering tree—the tree of life.

WHERE GIANTS DWELL

The story behind the Salish Sea's remarkable biodiversity begins in the magnificent coniferous forests that cloak the seaward slopes of the Vancouver Island Range and the Coast, Cascade, and Olympic Mountains. Lush and prolific, these temperate rainforests are the creation of wind-driven moisture gathered from the vast fetch of the Pacific Ocean. Optimal growing conditions—high precipitation, the moderating influence of a maritime climate, and nutrient-rich soils—give the conifer species that dominate these watershed forests the potential to reach enormous size and live for hundreds and even a thousand years or more.

Join a group of "arbornauts" aboard one of the giant construction cranes now being used by forest biologists to explore the dynamic world of the forest canopy. From a vantage point deep in the midst of the old-growth canopy, we see an irregular green skyline with a few skyscraping trees towering above the others. These are the forest elders, and most were already standing tall when Juan de Fuca sailed into the Salish Sea in 1592. One of these trees, a Douglas fir, is 750 years old and 300 feet (91m) tall. Nearby, a western red cedar is at least 1,000 years old and more than 200 feet (61m) tall with a basal girth of at least 20 feet (6m). The rainforests surrounding the Salish Sea are as unique as the sea itself because nearly every conifer found here is the tallest of its kind on the planet.

Our ancient conifers are forest sentinels with stories to tell—each one attesting to the wonder of

Western red cedar is the sacred "tree of life" for the Coast Salish, prized for the bounty it has always provided. Every remaining grove is a sacred and venerable place. Although old-growth red cedar is still being cut in British Columbia, it is largely gone from Washington except in state and federal parks and preserves.

Hunting by night, a bobcat traverses a downed cedar as it hunts for voles and squirrels on the forest floor.

evolution and life's ability to adapt. To understand how these trees grew to be such giants, forest biologists studied their internal architecture and discovered that Pacific Northwest conifers have an unusual abundance of cellular storage reservoirs in their conducting sapwood. The trunk of a mature western hemlock, for example, is a marvel of biological engineering, as evidenced by its ability to store thousands of gallons (liters) of water in its sapwood. In addition, the hemlock's branches are festooned with as many as 70 million needles, all capturing sunlight to power photosynthesis on a grand scale.

Dipper nests, typically consisting of well-camouflaged balls of living moss, are situated on cliff ledges or tucked behind waterfalls to be inaccessible to most predators.

RIVER-WALKING SPRITE

There is only one truly aquatic songbird—the petite water sprite known as the American dipper. The dipper's distinctive song is a melodious wellspring of joy, delivered both summer and winter, blending the most beautiful notes of the thrushes and the wrens into a stunning repertoire that can easily be heard over the sound of rushing water.

This plump slate-gray bird is best known as an underwater river-walker, leaping or flying directly into a raging torrent. When completely submerged, dippers face upstream, angling their short wings so that the current keeps them on the bottom while they forage. They use their long legs and big unwebbed feet to walk along the stony streambed, searching under rocks for water insects, larvae, fish eggs, and the tiniest of fish.

Dippers will also "fly" underwater, just like seabirds do, when the water is deep enough. On a favorite boulder in midstream, they will bob up and down and do the dipper version of knee bends—about 40 to 60 bobs a minute.

Dippers have evolved an astonishing array of anatomical and physiological aids for underwater foraging in fast-moving cold water. Their mostly spherical shape—very short tail and almost neckless body—is an adaptation to reduce the overall surface area available for heat loss in frigid water. Dippers are also well insulated by a dense plumage underlaid with down, all of which is heavily waterproofed with oil from a preen gland 10 times larger than that of any other similarly sized songbird. Only when higher elevation waters ice over

Winters in the Pacific Northwest are generally mild and extremely wet, with at least 75 percent of the total annual moisture falling from late fall to early spring. In addition to rain and snow, clouds and fog often shroud the Salish Sea and the mountains in a moist, wintry embrace. In contrast to growing conditions in other temperate rainforests, summers in the Pacific Northwest tend to be sunny, warm, and exceedingly dry—a climate pattern that imposes a virtual drought on our coastal forests when the water demands of the growing season are at peak levels. For these conifer species, immense size, both in height and girth, clearly offers the advantage of maximizing the sheer volume of cellular space available for water storage during times of water scarcity.

All life, plants and animals alike, requires nitrogen to biomanufacture proteins. This simple fact forms the basis for many of the relationships that we see in nature. Nitrogen, however, is virtually absent from the highly acidic water-leached soils of our coastal rainforests. When you stand in a coastal rainforest, you soon notice that the trees themselves and nearly everything on the forest floor are draped with lichens and mosses. On a mature Douglas fir, for example, at least one-fifth of the tree's foliage biomass consists of a single species of epiphytic lichen (*Lobaria oregano*) that contains nitrogen-fixing bacteria. Each time it rains, this vital protein building block is transferred—drop by drop—to the forest floor.

in winter do dippers shift their foraging to lower elevation intertidal streams. These amazing little birds have flap-covered nostrils that clamp down tightly to keep out water, much like the rubber nose plugs used by competitive swimmers. Dippers also store more oxygen in their blood than most other diving birds, which allows them to swim or dive up to 20 feet (6m) without coming up for air. Silvery-feathered membranes that pull up over their eyes effectively shield them from waterborne detritus or waterfall spray. The American dipper is truly a master of the air and the water!

The common raven is found from higher elevation forests to the shores of the Salish Sea.

43

The distinctive monotone whistle of a varied thrush is haunting and unmistakable. This beautiful forest-loving bird prefers nesting habitat in large unfragmented coniferous forests. In fall and winter, varied thrushes join robins and cedar waxwings foraging on the luscious orange berries of the madrone tree.

BURIED TREASURE

Trees are capable of manufacturing the entire spectrum of complex molecules needed for growth. But most trees and vascular plants couldn't exist without forming a mutually beneficial, or symbiotic, partnership with fungi. Fossil evidence suggests that land plants probably originated through a symbiosis between marine fungi and photosynthesizing algae at least 400 million years ago. The carpet of sphagnum and other mosses on the forest floor filters rainwater and protects the vast and matted network of fungal filaments, called mycelia, which thrive in the uppermost soil layers. This fungal mycelium assists trees and other plants with the uptake of nutrients, the absorption of water, and the promotion of organic decay. In trade, trees and other fungi-dependent green plants provide their fungal partners with sugars created as a by-product of photosynthesis in their leaves or needles.

The most remarkable of all symbiotic partnerships occurs when a tree root and its host-specific fungus combine to form mycorrhizae, a single organism that envelops tree roots and root hairs in a gauzelike layer that greatly enhances the tree's ability to extract water and critical nutrients from the soil. Western hemlocks are so dependent on mycorrhizal fungi that their roots barely penetrate the soil even as their trunks reach to the sky.

For this system to work, the fungus must reproduce and disperse its spores. The buried treasure of truffles and the colorful array of mushrooms that appear on logs and in the forest duff are the fungi's reproductive structures—all that we normally see of the gossamer mycorrhizal network. The earthy pungent aroma emanating from a buried truffle attracts a variety of mushroom connoisseurs, especially red-backed voles and squirrels. As these small mammals move about the forest, they scatter their feces—compact capsules containing fungal spores, yeast culture, and nitrogen-fixing bacteria—everything needed to inoculate roots and ensure the success of the next generation of mycorrhizae.

Fungi and a multitude of insects immediately work on dying or dead trees, every bit of woody tissue providing the recyclers with a diet rich in carbohydrates and nutrients. Rotting stumps and logs play a key role as "nurse" trees, providing the perfect conditions for the sprouting and survival of tree seedlings. In essence, forest soils are a terrestrial ocean—an important source of nutrients for the Salish Sea.

The charismatic and elusive spotted owl, shown at its cavity nest with its single young, is a forest ghost that has come to symbolize what is at stake if we lose the remaining stands of magnificent old-growth forest.

The legendary ability of wild salmon returning to the river or stream of their birth to spawn after years at sea is an evolutionary marvel. These sockeye salmon are homing on the unique chemistry of their natal waters and other physical attributes of the stream.

SALMON FEED THE FOREST

Pacific salmon are responsible for the Salish Sea's supreme gift to our watershed forests and estuaries: a virtual tsunami of nutrients carried from the ocean to the forest by salmon. The Salish Sea is unique because all 5 species of spawning Pacific salmon—chinook, coho, sockeye, chum, and pink—return by the thousands to their natal streams in these forests. Their arrival in freshwater streams and rivers provides a bountiful feast for bears, bald eagles, ravens, gulls, dippers, river otters, pine martens, and many smaller creatures, such as insects and amphibians.

Most salmon species put on at least 99 percent of their total weight during the 2 to 5 years they spend at sea, so the bodies of adult salmon reflect marine-derived nitrogen as opposed to nitrogen from terrestrial sources. Isotopes of marine-derived nitrogen are readily identifiable in plant and animal tissues. Tom Reimchen and a group of British Columbia scientists began tracking nitrogen uptake in coastal

When black bears fish for salmon, they contribute to the circle of life by which salmon-derived nitrogen nourishes the forest and the sea.

When spawning, the female salmon lies on her side and lashes her tail to lift streambed cobbles into the current, eventually scouring out a shallow depression, called a "red," in which she will lay her eggs.

OF FOG LARKS AND ANCIENT TREES

Wherever old-growth forests meet the shores of the Salish Sea, you might see robin-sized seabirds—marbled murrelets—riding the gentle swells offshore. Marbled murrelets are members of the auk family (the Alcidae), which includes the tufted puffin, rhinoceros auklet, pigeon guillemot, and the common murre. The species' common name refers to its breeding season plumage, which is a subtle marbled tapestry of chestnut brown and ivory; winter plumage is distinctly black and white. Like all alcids, marbled murrelets are superbly engineered for flying underwater in pursuit of tiny fish and other prey. They have short and very muscular wings, legs situated well back on the body, small webbed feet, a tiny tail, and dense waterproofed plumage. Marbled murrelets are capable of diving up to 44.8 feet (13.7m), deftly propelling themselves through the water by using their wings like flippers; their feet are used only for steering. Like all alcids, marbled murrelets have difficulty taking off from land. Once airborne, they fly with a blur of rapid wingbeats and without gliding.

The marbled murrelet is unique among alcids because its life is tied to the sea and the forest—an atypical lifestyle that evolved within the protective embrace of the majestic coniferous forests of the Pacific Rim. In contrast to colonial nesters like the rhinoceros auklet and the tufted puffin, the marbled murrelet is a solitary nester with a profound preference for old-growth forests as breeding habitat. The marbled murrelet is such a capable long-distance commuter that it will fly up to 40 miles (64km) from its foraging areas at sea to its nest tree if the forest habitat is right. In fact, loggers called these seabirds "fog larks" because their plaintive high-pitched *keer-keer* vocalizations were a haunting presence in coastal logging camps.

Most forest-nesting birds make use of tree cavities or build a well-constructed nest in the fork of a branch. Marbled murrelets have webbed feet that are poorly suited to nest building or moving about on branches in the forest canopy. Although a few nests have been found on the forest floor, most marbled murrelet nests consist of a simple depression in a cushion of moss and lichens on a thick, horizontal tree limb; no other nesting materials are added. Only very old trees, at least 150 years or more, provide these types of nesting sites, which limits the murrelet's choices to old-growth forests. Also in contrast to other alcid species, the murrelet's brownish breeding-season plumage and its greenish-tinted spotted egg are consistent with adaptations exhibited by other forest-nesting birds and provides camouflage that reduces the risk of being spotted by aerial predators.

Marbled murrelet eggs are the size of chicken eggs—considered large for such a small bird. Incubation, shared by both adults, takes about 30 days. The nestling period of about 28 days is also long by alcid standards, but young marbled murrelets must be fully developed and capable of sustained flight—all the way to the sea—before they leave the nest. That first fateful takeoff from such a high nest must be a bit like hang gliding—a scary free fall until the wings get pumping and the juvenile murrelet careens through the maze of trees keeping up with its parents. Once safely at sea, the young bird will join its parents and other murrelets, but it still must forage on its own.

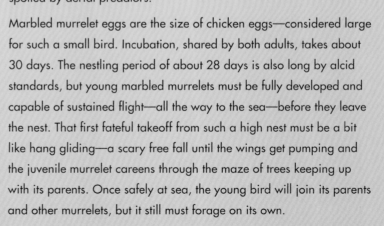

Winter plumage

Summer plumage

Steelhead are rainbow trout that spend 2 to 3 years at sea before returning to their native river to spawn. However, unlike Pacific salmon, they do not die after spawning and will migrate back to the ocean to feed before returning to the same river to spawn again.

forests decades ago. What they and other researchers working in Washington discovered is that salmon-derived nitrogen is profoundly important to the nutrient cycle that nourishes both the forest and the sea.

Salmon-derived nitrogen is present in all trophic levels of our watershed forests and estuaries—in the soil, in needles at the top of giant conifers, in all types of streamside vegetation, and in the tissues of birds, mammals, and insects that feed on salmon. Studies have shown that 138 species of terrestrial and marine vertebrates and countless invertebrates are dependent on salmon. In streams and rivers, salmon carcasses and detrital bits "fertilize" freshwater systems all the way to the sea. In fact, it has been demonstrated that there is a direct correlation between the amount of marine-derived nitrogen in a tree's annual growth rings and the size of the year's salmon run. The ecological relationship between salmon and an astonishing diversity of life forms, plant and animal alike, is unique in the natural world. Just as salmon feed the forests, the trees of the forest, in turn, take care of salmon by maintaining stream habitat complexity and by providing critical shade. Although they are neither salty nor wet, the forests surrounding the Salish Sea are a critical part of the Salish Sea.

When the tide is out, the table is set.

—Coast Salish saying

Life at the Edges

Great blue herons are stealth opportunists, adapting their tai chi slow-motion hunting style to suit the chosen habitat and prey. With its daggerlike bill, this heron has captured a greenling.

◄ Coastal edges—where land and sea meet—are exciting places to explore. You do not have to be a diver to enjoy the intertidal wilderness, as this sunset at Sucia Island in the San Juan Islands attests. Wherever you look, you will discover life's infinite capacity for beauty and diversity.

Along the edges of the Salish Sea, the twice-daily ebb and flood of the tides shape the rhythm of life. Marine plants and animals that live in the intertidal zone—areas along the shore that are submerged at high tide and exposed at low tide—must adapt to life in the sea and on land in order to survive. The oxygen that most marine animals need is dissolved in seawater, so when the tide is out, they must keep their body tissues moist by burrowing into wet mud or sand, or by seeking shelter beneath rocks and various types of seaweed. Air breathers crossing the high-tide line from land must carry their oxygen supply with them. At low tide, when there is little or no food available for intertidal animals, they must adapt by alternating between periods of activity and quiescence. Whether the preferred habitat is muddy ooze, sand, cobble, or a rock-rimmed tidepool, the activities required to maintain life are usually conducted when the tide is in. In the nurturing balance that has evolved over time, what the sea takes away from the intertidal zone it gives back in plenitude, delivering the gift of food and oxygen with every incoming wave.

51

BEAVER DAMS: DAMNED SAFE PLACES FOR SALMON

Greg Hood, a biologist with the Skagit River System Cooperative, discovered beavers make dams and lodges in the tidal shrub zone of the Skagit River delta (left) that are smaller than beaver dams and lodges in freshwater (below). At high tide, the smaller beaver dams are usually under 3 feet (1m) or more of water, but when the tide ebbs, the dams maintain enough water in the channels for beaver to swim as well as for fish (juvenile chinook salmon, for example) to hide from predators. And those dams make damned safe places: three times as many juvenile chinook can be found in low-tide pools created by beaver dams as in tidal channels not altered by beavers.

QUIET BAYS, MUDFLATS, AND SALT MARSHES

In quiet, relatively shallow waters—wind-sheltered bays and broad deltas that form at the mouths of major rivers like the Fraser or the Skagit—low tide reveals worlds that are unknown to most of us. To the casual beach walker, a mudflat at low tide may seem devoid of life, but the strange holes, mounds, and corkscrew-shaped excrescences that pattern the surface hint at a hidden world that flourishes just beneath the surface. Explore an estuary slough, and you might discover a salmon nursery in the warm saltgrass-shaded waters where hundreds of salmon fry congregate to feast on the bounty of tiny invertebrates. Nearby, you are likely to spot a statue-still hunter—a great blue heron—waiting patiently for the unwary fry or starry flounder to swim within range of its lightning-fast bill.

Sediment-rich intertidal habitats are extraordinarily important to the Salish Sea food web, providing ideal living conditions for a remarkable diversity of burrowing filter feeders, including hardshell and softshell clams, oysters, ghost shrimp, amphipods, snails, and marine worms. On a rising tide, burrowing species may actually come to the surface, others will thrust their long siphon tubes into the food-rich current, and some will begin filter feeding by pumping water through their burrows. When the tide ebbs, mud and sand dwellers withdraw into the deep wet layers. Shallow pools and sloughs that retain water provide spawning habitat for surf smelt and sand lance, as well as nursery corridors for juvenile salmon. Thousands of migratory shorebirds, as well as resident birds (such as crows, great blue herons, sandhill cranes, and gulls), all depend on the remarkable diversity of food resources available in soft sediments. As the Coast Salish would say: "When the tide is out, the table is set."

A glaucous-winged gull is engaged in a standoff with a feisty kelp crab. The Salish Sea hosts 16 species of gulls, including glaucous-winged (the only year-round resident), western, Bonaparte's, Heermann's, herring, and mew. Gulls take several years to mature. The plumage of juveniles is light brown or mottled; with age, gulls develop lustrous white plumage with gray or black areas on the wings or body, depending on the species.

TIDEPOOLS AND ROCKY REEFS

Resplendent against rockweed (left) and sea lettuce–edged pools (above), these dazzling ochre and purple sea stars (all the same species: *Pisaster ochraceus*) would steal the show on any tidepool walk. Ochre stars are generalists. As carnivores, they savor mussels but also forage in lower intertidal habitats for barnacles, snails, small crabs, and other shellfish. Using the tiny tube feet on its arms to move about, a sea star locates and consumes its prey by engulfing it in the bag-like stomach it extrudes through the oral opening on the underside of its body. Juices secreted by the sea star's stomach dissolve the prey's body tissues. The resulting liquid is absorbed like a seafood smoothie.

Exploring a tidepool brings out the child in all of us. Rocky reefs and rockbound shorelines are dynamic high-energy environments influenced by strong currents and tidal action. Living between the tides is stressful enough, but the marine animals and plants that thrive in these habitats must be able to live out of water for many hours at a time, tolerate intense summer sun and winter nighttime cold, and be able to hold their own when the tide-driven surf reclaims their rocky substrate. The upper limit of existence for intertidal species is dominated by dense populations of a very few tolerant species, whereas the exquisite beauty and diversity of the low intertidal zone is mind boggling.

When you look closely at the biggest rocks that extend above a tidepool, you'll notice that several species of algae, barnacles, and mollusks are arranged in horizontal bands. The black encrusting tar lichen delineates the highest splash zone, where you can see that the lichen crust and algal film are being actively grazed by hordes of periwinkle snails. Just below this band is a dense encrustation of acorn barnacles, the highest-growing and most desiccation-tolerant of the barnacle species. And just beneath the acorn barnacle zone is the middle intertidal zone where mussels and dog whelks predominate; the mussels loosen the barnacles by crowding them out, and the whelks feast on the dislodged barnacles. Mussels attach themselves to the rocks with leathery threads secreted from a gland in their "foot," filtering planktonic animals from the seawater that washes over them and delivering these organisms to their mouths by way of mucus- and cilia-covered gills. The largest residents of the lower intertidal zone are the sea stars, relentless predators whose hydrostatic skeletons stiffen to absorb the impact of the surf and then soften to allow the hydraulically powered tube feet to move the animals from place to place.

AN ARRAY OF ANEMONES

More than a dozen species of anemones can be found in both intertidal and subtidal habitats of the Salish Sea.

Painted anemone (above left) and close-up with black-and-white sea fleas (above right).

White-spotted anemone open (above left) and closed (above right).

Pink-tipped anemones that have a unicellular symbiotic alga called Chorella living in the anemone's skin will have a green color (top). Those without the symbiotic alga will not (below).

Strawberry anemones (right) and pink-tipped anemones (left and above left) can reproduce by dividing asexually. As an individual anemone divides, the two halves slowly crawl away from each other until they eventually split into two genetically identical clones. This type of reproduction allows anemones to rapidly use available space and exclude competing species, helps to protect against predatory nudibranchs, and can permit the capture of prey much larger than a single anemone could ever hold.

At low tide, a rock-rimmed tidepool is a magical world. From above, the emerald-hued waters in a rockbound cove look almost tropical. At the tidepool's edge, you can see a mesmerizing mosaic of jewel-like colors—the apricot-rose of coralline algae, serpentine-green anemones, amethyst-hued sea urchins, ochre-colored sea stars, and sea cucumbers the color of fire agates. Luminous green sea lettuce intermixed with bronzed bouquets of rockweed drape the edges of this marine rock garden. Slowly, perfectly camouflaged animals begin to reveal themselves. Gently lift up a rock, and you might surprise a purple shore crab or catch a glimpse of a tidepool sculpin. Exploring a Salish Sea tidepool is addictive, and soon, just like a marine biologist, you will be marking the dates of the lowest tides on your calendar.

Hermit crabs use the empty shells of snails, whelks, and other univalves as portable houses and protection from predators. The orange hermit crab uses its large right claw as a door to seal off the shell when withdrawing inside.

Goose neck barnacles, generally found in dense aggregations in the surf zone, thrive on near-vertical wave-washed rocks. Because goose necks are taller than their competitors, they are better situated to filter food from wave runoff.

The cryptically colored penpoint gunnel, usually less than 10 inches (25cm) in length, is a denizen of seaweed-filled tidepools found under barnacle-encrusted rocks exposed in the low-tide zone or the nearshore subtidal area.

Black oystercatchers are year-round residents of rocky mid-tide and high-tide zones. Their bright red bills, long pink legs and feet, coal-black bodies, and raucous calls make them the easiest of all shorebirds to identify. Oystercatchers use their long bills to probe seaweed-clad rock outcroppings for snails, periwinkles, limpets, small mussels, and marine worms. Despite their name, they do not really "catch" or eat oysters.

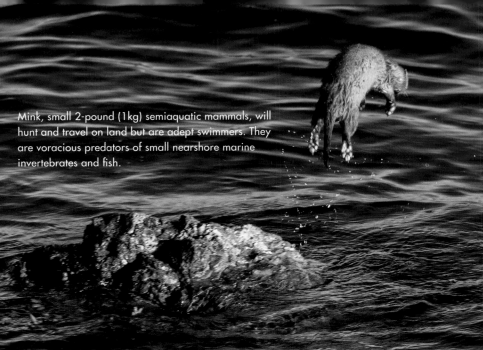

Mink, small 2-pound (1kg) semiaquatic mammals, will hunt and travel on land but are adept swimmers. They are voracious predators of small nearshore marine invertebrates and fish.

Weighing up to 24 pounds (11kg), river otters (right) are substantially larger than mink (above) and are much better swimmers and divers. Although they prey on nesting birds and consume invertebrates like kelp crabs, river otters prefer fish and tend to catch mostly slow-moving fish, such as gunnels, sculpins, and pricklebacks. Unrelated male river otters may form packs and hunt cooperatively, which increases their success at capturing faster-moving but more nutritious forage fish (herring and sand lance, for example).

One of the best-kept secrets about the Salish Sea is that from dawn to dusk, there is always something happening in the intertidal zone. While Salish Sea waters are home to a fascinating group of marine mammals, about 25 percent of the 38 species of mammals that depend on the sea for food or other critical resources live mostly on land. These mammals, including black-tailed deer, red fox, both black and brown bear, mink, river otter, beaver, and muskrat, are frequently seen by people exploring the array of freshwater and saltwater habitats along our coastal edges.

Birds—great blue herons, gulls, northwestern crows, ravens, short-eared owls, and belted kingfishers, for example—and many shorebirds are also frequent visitors to these important habitats. Some mammals and birds play a critical role as scavengers, taking advantage of what the tide delivers or the tasty bits left behind by previous diners. Many are opportunistic hunters that relish the bounty that the Salish Sea delivers. Although we may exploit these food resources in different ways than our mammal or bird neighbors do, our dependency on the biological productivity and health of the Salish Sea is no less profound.

A glaucous-winged gull, foraging intertidally, will eat anything that can fit in its bill, including an ochre sea star.

The body shape and behavior of the hooded nudibranch bears little resemblance to that of other sea slug species. The translucent 3- to 4-inch-long (8 to 10cm) body and the inflated hood of inward-pointing tentacles suggest a marine version of a Venus flytrap. Clinging to a blade of eelgrass and waving in the current, the nudibranch uses its fringed hood like a net, snapping it shut to snare zooplankton, small crustaceans, and even tiny fish. The buoyancy of the hood is further enhanced as it entraps carbon dioxide and other gases, which enable the nudibranch to swim more easily to new foraging positions.

OCEAN GARDENS: EELGRASS BEDS

All anemones start life as females, developing testes only as they mature. Brooding anemones are unusual in that once the anemone's eggs are fertilized by waterborne sperm, the eggs undergo initial development within the mother's gastrovascular cavity until they are ready to be expelled as a mucus-covered mass. Once released, the egg mass slides down the mother's body column and adheres to its base; the young anemones continue to develop their ring of tentacles until they can move away and live independently.

Ocean gardens occur on the threshold of the deeper sea—the subtidal zone—where forests of bull kelp reach for the sun and animals "bloom" like flowers. Beds of eelgrass play a key role in maintaining the biological productivity and environmental health of Salish Sea ecosystems. This narrow-leaved flowering plant blooms beneath the waves and sends clouds of pollen drifting with the currents. Eelgrass is found in shallow offshore waters and grows preferentially on sandy or muddy areas of the seafloor. Each leaf blade acts as a small food factory, supporting a living film of diatoms, bacteria, and other microscopic organisms that will, in turn, serve as food for larger invertebrates. Beds of eelgrass, whether living or dead, play a critical role in providing food and shelter for a great variety of invertebrate and vertebrate species, including hooded nudibranchs, aggregating anemones, kelp crabs, and fish such as salmon, lingcod, Pacific herring, sand lance, and many other species. Because of their importance as fish nurseries, these underwater prairies provide foraging areas for birds, salmon, herring, seals, sea lions, and whales. Eelgrass beds also absorb massive amounts of carbon dioxide from the atmosphere and function as carbon sinks for greenhouse gases. On a warm, sunny day, if you lower a hydrophone into a bed of eelgrass, you will hear the champagne-like bubbling sound emanating from the plant as it absorbs and photosynthesizes.

▲ Hooded nudibranchs congregate along fronds of kelp.

Sea palm kelp (*Postelsia palmaeformis*) may resemble a tiny palm tree, but its habitat is anything but tropical. This spectacular annual is restricted to wave-exposed headlands where it outcompetes mussels and barnacles in securing its space on the rocks.

UNDERSEA FORESTS

Forests of burnished-bronze bull kelp and northern giant kelp, waving in the current, are among the most beautiful and productive ecosystems in the sea. Bull kelp is an annual species, attaching its holdfast to a rock and sending up a stalk that may reach 65 feet (20m) in length in a single summer. From a bulbous float at the top of the stalk, the broad, flat blades up to 8 inches (20cm) wide and as long as 10 feet (3m) fan out into the current. In late summer, each plant produces over a trillion zoospores before it dies; great windrows of bull kelp intertwined with other seaweeds wash up on Salish Sea beaches each winter, providing food and shelter for invertebrates as well as forage for black-tailed deer.

◄ Kelp forests have both an understory and a canopy, which provide structural diversity attractive to an array of animals found nowhere else in the Salish Sea. These wave-moderating forests provide optimal habitat for abalone, shield-backed kelp crabs, red sea urchins, kelp greenling, kelp perch, and Pacific herring.

The egg-yolk jellyfish, a cnidarian the size of a soccer ball, cruises near the water's surface. It can often be seen near large aggregations of moon jellies on which it feeds. In the summer and early fall, graceful larval and juvenile rock crabs will sometimes hitch a ride on this jelly's bell or on one of its oral arms.

Biological diversity—
"biodiversity" in the new parlance—
is the key to the maintenance of the world
as we know it.

—E. O. Wilson

Denizens of the Deep

The abundance and diversity of marine life in the Salish Sea is astonishing. Invertebrates—animals without backbones—come in every size imaginable from the microscopic to the macroscopic. People do not generally think of invertebrates when speaking about "world's largest," but the Salish Sea is home to some of the world's largest invertebrates, including the geoduck (world's largest burrowing clam), gumboot chiton (world's largest chiton), giant barnacle (world's largest barnacle), giant plumose anemone (world's tallest anemone), and giant Pacific octopus (world's largest octopus). You get the picture, but even the invertebrates that do not qualify as record-holding members of the Salish Sea's huge cast of invertebrates are fascinating.

◀ The diatom *Chaetoceros debilis* is one of the many microscopic plankton found in the Salish Sea that uses photosynthesis to convert the sun's energy into chemical energy.

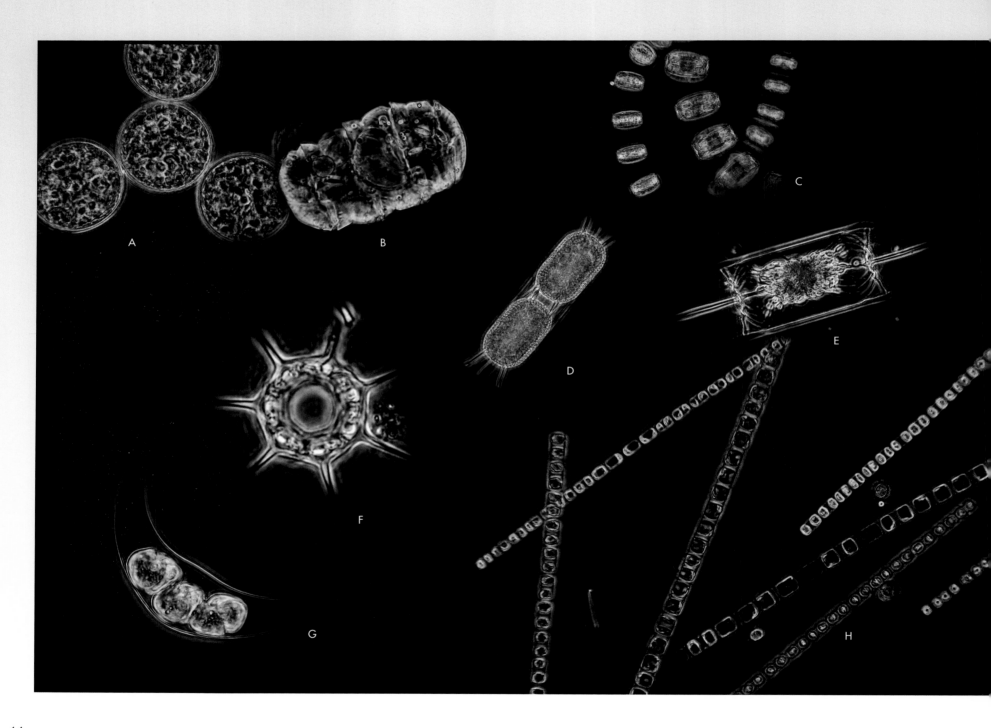

INVISIBLE TO THE NAKED EYE, BUT ESSENTIAL

I

When viewed through a microscope, plankton species in the Salish Sea are as diverse as snowflakes.

A *Actinoptychus*

B *Polykrikos schwartzii*

C *Thalassiosira*

D *Corethron*

E *Ditylum brightwellii*

F *Dictyoca speculum*

G *Dissodinium pseudolunula*

H *Skeletonema costatum*

I *Thalassionema*

J *Corethron*

K *Odontella*

J

Some scientists speculate that there are likely more than 3,000 species of macro-invertebrates in the Salish Sea—and those are only the ones you can see with your bare eyes. It's not likely anyone would venture a guess on the number of microscopic invertebrate species found in the Salish Sea, but we know they play a critical role in the sea's food web.

Many people consider phytoplankton to be plants rather than invertebrate animals, but they are so important to the ecosystem, we would be remiss to not give them their due honors. Microscopic photosynthetic plankton are autotrophs. These single-celled microalgae and photosynthetic bacteria combine the sun's energy with nutrients brought into the Salish Sea from the depths of the outer ocean and upland areas to grow and create the foundation for the food web. These phytoplankton are consumed by zooplankton (which are definitely invertebrates), and the complex web of who eats whom moves upward and expands outward until you reach the charismatic megavertebrates at the top—humans, killer whales, bald eagles, and so on.

K

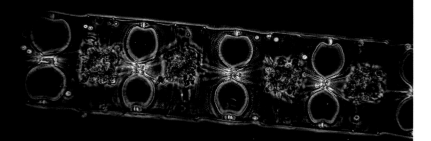

A daisy brittle star strikes a beautiful contrast to the iridescent violet color of blue branching seaweed, known as *Fauchea laciniata*, which strangely enough is in the red-algae family.

◀ One of the largest crab species in the Salish Sea, the juvenile Puget Sound king crab (standing on encrusting hydrocoral) can have a shell width of 1 foot (30cm).

The solitary stubby squid does not school as market squid do.

PICK A FAVORITE

Of the 3,000 Salish Sea marine invertebrates that you can easily see, you might pick a favorite. If you are fond of superlatives, the giant Pacific octopus might be your choice. How many suckers does it have? Isn't it inspiring that the female can lay 100,000 eggs and spend 9 months caring for them, only to die after the eggs hatch? If you favor economics, the geoduck or Dungeness crab might be good choices, as both are foundations for multimillion-dollar fisheries in the Salish Sea. Those fascinated with history might consider the northern abalone, the Salish Sea's only species of abalone. These gastropods have been harvested and eaten, and their beautiful shells have been traded by some groups of Coast Salish since time immemorial. If you like diversity, you might pick a beautiful nudibranch, then pick another, and another. If you're a foodie, choose the spot prawn. There is not a lobster in the world that will stand up to the taste of a fresh, locally harvested spot prawn. And spot prawns are caught in pots, which minimizes the bycatch and destructive seafloor issues associated with shrimp harvest in other parts of the world. And if you are into cute, by all means choose the stubby squid. Invertebrates don't get any cuter than this one!

SYMBIOTIC RELATIONSHIPS

There are numerous accounts of symbiosis between invertebrates in the Salish Sea. One example, perhaps as well known for how pleasing it is to the eye as for its biological relationship, is the symbiosis between the crimson anemone and the candy stripe shrimp. Deep inside the beautifully red-banded tentacles of this crimson anemone is an equally beautiful shrimp distinctively marked with bands of red, yellow, and blue.

The candy stripe shrimp feeds primarily on material egested by the anemone as well as on dead tissue sloughed off the anemone; at the same time, the shrimp protects the anemone from other creatures (the Snyder blade shrimp, for example) that will pick at and damage the tips of the crimson anemone's tentacles.

A school of market squid at night.

KNOWING, NOT JUST IDENTIFYING

Many of the fascinating invertebrates lie beneath the Salish Sea, but you do not have to take up scuba diving to see them. Visit the beach during low tide and explore the intertidal, waiting and watching tidepools for movement; gently turn rocks—and replace them, of course. You will be amazed at the variety of organisms you find. Don't make the mistake of thinking you "know" an invertebrate simply because you can identify it. Learn what it eats, what eats it, and the special adaptations that help it survive. You will soon discover that the lives of your marine invertebrate neighbors are every bit as intricate as your own. Most people take their low-tide walks midday during the summer, but remember that in the Salish Sea, extreme low tides also occur at night during the winter. Bundle up, put on your headlamp, and get out there.

▲ Possibly one of the Salish Sea's most spectacular snails, this jeweled top snail is searching for hydroids, its preferred prey, amid orange cup coral.

Anemones are often thought of as sedentary, but when a leather sea star approaches a swimming anemone, the anemone will rise up, rapidly bend down, sting the star (you might call this act head-butting if anemones had heads), release itself from the seafloor, and then swim away to escape being eaten.

SUPER SUCKERS

Sometimes weighing as much as 150 pounds (68kg), the Salish Sea's giant Pacific octopus is the largest octopus in the world. Generally timid and retiring, the giant Pacific octopus has been documented to have attacked scuba divers on rare occasions.

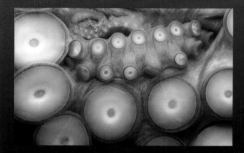

The invertebrate icon of the Salish Sea, this octopus has 2,240 suckers: 280 on each of its 8 arms. That is, if it is a female. Males only have 2,060 suckers, as their third right arm (the hectocotylized arm, or the modified arm—the one they use to inseminate females) has only 100 suckers. If someone asks how many suckers there are on a giant Pacific octopus, be sure to clarify, "Male or female?"

Giant Pacific octopus

SOFT-BODIED AND NAKED

Soft-bodied and naked, nudibranchs, or sea slugs with "naked gills," as their name suggests, are easy to fall in love with. Their diverse assortment of electric colors, often paired in striking contrasts, combined with their varied anatomy, or "architecture," would have impressed even Antonio Gaudi. Their bold coloration carries a warning: *Beware my poisonous and unpalatable nature.* Members of one nudibranch subgroup, known as the aeolids, are able to feed on anemones, but instead of being injured by the anemone's stinging nematocysts, they can ingest and transport the intact stinging cells to their own outer layer for protection. Pretty and clever!

A Red flabellina, or
   predaceous aeolis

B Sea lemon

C Opalescent
   nudibranch

D Cockerell's
   nudibranch

E Clown nudibranch

73

Salmon are unique because their symbolic power and their economic value have survived together to the threshold of the twenty-first century. And this holds the best hope for salmon and the people who need them.

—Carl Safina

◄ A giant barnacle nestled among strawberry anemones uses its cirri to scoop plankton from the water into its mouth.

Bizarre and Beautiful Fish

Tropical coral reefs bring to mind an array of colorful fish in every shape and size, but this diversity is not what most people imagine they will see in the cold temperate waters of the Salish Sea. Instead of color and diversity, they expect murky green water and drab gray fish, which couldn't be further from the truth. The Salish Sea is home to a grand assortment—253 species, to be exact—of exquisitely colorful and fascinating fish.

The beautiful elongate pectoral fins of a grunt sculpin are better suited for "walking" over rocks or the seafloor than they are for swimming. The fins also help camouflage grunt sculpins when they hide in the empty shells of giant barnacles, where the pectoral fins (and tail) mimic the cirri, or multi-segmented leg-like appendages, that a giant barnacle uses to scoop plankton from the water column into its mouth.

75

SALMON NATION

To a great extent, salmon define the Salish Sea, unique for being the southernmost latitude at which all 5 species of Pacific salmon still run wild. Called anadromous by scientists, chinook, chum, coho, pink, and sockeye salmon hatch from eggs laid in the gravel of freshwater streams and rivers and migrate into saltwater where they grow into adults. Variation, both between and within species, is the word to remember when pondering the salmon life cycle. After hatching, some juvenile salmon (all pink and chum, some chinook) will migrate from freshwater to saltwater rather quickly, while others (all sockeye, almost all coho, and some chinook) might spend 1 or 2 years in freshwater lakes prior to out-migrating to saltwater. Once in saltwater, they also differ in the amount of time spent in the nearshore and open ocean habitat before returning to natal rivers and streams to spawn. For all 5 species, spawning is their only act of love, as they will die after laying or fertilizing eggs.

The Salish Sea also boasts 3 other closely related anadromous fish species that are born in freshwater but will migrate into saltwater to feed and grow. Sea-run cutthroat, steelhead, and bull trout, however, can survive spawning and make multiple trips between freshwater and saltwater.

Male salmon, like this coho, will develop a hooked snout, as its genus *Oncorhynchus* indicates, when it returns to spawn.

▲ Everybody knows that seals eat salmon, but that is just the tip of the salmon gourmet iceberg. It is doubtful that there is any other group of species that supports the number of invertebrate and vertebrate species that salmon do between all their life stages from freshwater to saltwater and even after they have spawned and died. One researcher calculated that 138 species of terrestrial and marine mammals, birds, reptiles, and amphibians currently or historically common to the Salish Sea area depend on salmon.

Despite their astonishing colors, shapes, and sizes, most fish species in the Salish Sea are found elsewhere in northern Pacific waters. Biologists use the term *endemic* to describe species that occur only in a certain place or ecosystem and nowhere else. There are very few endemic fish species in the Salish Sea because the marine ecosystem is relatively new, both geologically and biologically speaking. But we do know that many of the fish species in the Salish Sea are genetically distinct—a sure sign of evolution in progress.

The copper rockfish is only one of the Salish Sea's 27 long-lived rockfish species, all of which are in the scorpionfish family. Like others in this family, rockfish have venom in the tissue that lines grooves in their dorsal, anal, and pelvic spines.

Age—extreme age—is what you will find. Many of these species get very old: some even unbelievably old. Rougheye rockfish can live to be over 200 years, yelloweye rockfish 118, spiny dogfish 100, and quillback rockfish 90, just to name a few. Fisheries biologists consider a species to be long-lived if its maximum age is 30 or more. They even consider fish with maximum ages between 11 and 29 to be old because when compared to the ages of most of the fish we eat, they *are* old. For example, most salmon are about 3 or 4 years old when they return to the Salish Sea from the Pacific Ocean and are caught for the table. Why, beyond being fascinating, does longevity matter to fisheries biologists? Many long-lived fishes do not reproduce every year, so the adults have to live a long time to be able to have multiple successful reproductive years over their life span, meaning we need to harvest more sparingly and leave more in the wild. It is the job of fisheries biologists, after all, to help us understand how many fish we can catch to eat while ensuring that we don't take too many and cause the populations to collapse. And for those of us who are not fisheries biologists, knowing a fish might have been born when Woodrow Wilson was president is important because who would want to eat such a wily old survivor. Milton Love, a fish biologist at the University of California, Santa Barbara, claims one of the three immutable laws of the universe is "Never eat anything older than your grandmother."

OLDER THAN YOUR GRANDMOTHER?
Longevity Records for Some Salish Sea Species

COMMON NAME	LONGEVITY (YEARS)
Giant Pacific octopus	5
Snowy owl	10
Pigeon guillemot	11
North American river otter	12
Western grebe	13
Barrow's goldeneye	15
Pacific herring	15
Pelagic cormorant	17
Kelp greenling	18
White-winged scoter	18
Northern elephant seal	21
Glaucous-winged gull	22
Great blue heron	23
Lingcod	25
Common murre	26
Bald eagle	28
Harbor seal	29
Quillback rockfish	90
Spiny dogfish	100
Killer whale	103
Yelloweye rockfish	118
Geoduck	168
Red sea urchin	200
Rougheye rockfish	205

THE APTLY NAMED SAND LANCE

Sand lance, small plankton-eating fish, congregate in very large schools. These fat-filled fish are a favorite prey of numerous fish, bird, and mammal species throughout the Salish Sea. Like some other prey fish, sand lance escape from predators by hiding in the sand, but their technique is different. Most burrowing fish lie on the sand and wiggle their bodies like dancers in a mosh pit. This action throws a blizzard of sand up into the water column, which eventually settles on top of the fish. Not sand lance. According to Adam Summers, a research scientist at the University of Washington's Friday Harbor Laboratories, sand lance burrow face-first. Like a lance being plunged into the ground, the fish hits the sand with its snout while it undulates its tail vigorously, shoving its head and body into the seafloor. When about two-thirds of the fish's body is buried, the tail is still, and the sand lance seems to effortlessly slip into the sand. Emerging has to be an easier maneuver.

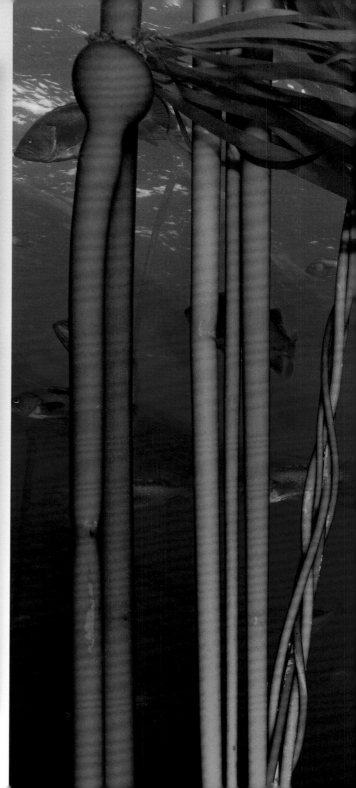

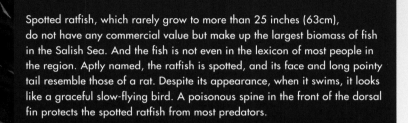

Spotted ratfish, which rarely grow to more than 25 inches (63cm), do not have any commercial value but make up the largest biomass of fish in the Salish Sea. And the fish is not even in the lexicon of most people in the region. Aptly named, the ratfish is spotted, and its face and long pointy tail resemble those of a rat. Despite its appearance, when it swims, it looks like a graceful slow-flying bird. A poisonous spine in the front of the dorsal fin protects the spotted ratfish from most predators.

THEN AND NOW: FISH WITH A PURPOSE

Fish are beauty with purpose. They play a multitude of roles in the Salish Sea's ecosystem and serve a utilitarian role for people: We love to eat them. Salmon are the spiritual food of the Coast Salish, and they have been caught, eaten, and revered by them since the Pleistocene glaciers receded and the first salmon swam into the Salish Sea. Herring also were, and still are, an important fish for many Coast Salish tribes and First Nations, especially in the northern Salish Sea. Archeological records suggest that salmon, herring, and herring eggs were consistently used by the Coast Salish over time, even through periods of large variations in ocean temperature and productivity. In contrast, in modern times, salmon and herring productivity vary quite a bit as ocean conditions change. Why was productivity, and consequently availability, so stable during historical Coast Salish use? It's not entirely clear, but the stability likely indicates a fine balance between the Coast Salish and the ecosystem—one that commercial harvest may have upset.

Coast Salish tribes and First Nations still harvest culturally, nutritionally, and economically important fish like salmon, herring, and halibut, but they now also share these resources with nontribal commercial and recreational fishermen, many of whom also define themselves by their love for these fish and their passion for fishing. Recreational fishing for salmon, lingcod, halibut, and other fish has been and will continue to be an economically and socially important feature of the Salish Sea.

Lingcod, with a face only a mother could love, will eat pretty much anything they can fit into their mouths, including other lingcod. Heavy strikers, good fighters on the line, large, and delicious, lingcod are an angler's dream and are fished throughout the rocky high-relief areas of the Salish Sea.

◄ Black rockfish school in groups and do not hesitate to move in pursuit of food. Individuals of other rockfish species, however, are homebodies, spending their entire adult lives in near solitude close to a favored small grouping of rocks.

Research suggests that the Salish Sea is used as a birthing site by pregnant bluntnose sixgill sharks and as a nursery area where juvenile sharks mature before moving into the open ocean.

BASKING SHARKS: THE STORY BEHIND THE PICTURE

In July 2009, marine biologist and famous underwater cinematographer Florian Graner was boating up the west side of San Juan Island, preparing for an afternoon of fieldwork. As he passed Salmon Bank, he noticed a pair of large crescent-shaped dorsal fins belonging to fish almost as long as his boat. Alone on his boat, Graner donned his bubble-free rebreathing scuba equipment, grabbed his camera, tethered himself to the boat with a long line, and slipped into the water with a pair of giant basking sharks, one of which was close to 26 feet (8m) long. Fortunately, he captured incredible video and still images of them with their giant mouths agape as they strained seawater through gill rakers—modified skin cells that cover the gills and filter copepods and other zooplankton—at a rate of 132,000 gallons (500,000l) of water per hour.

Once abundant in parts of the Salish Sea, basking sharks became a targeted fishery in British Columbia in 1949 when listed by the Canadian Federal Fisheries department as destructive pests because of their propensity to entangle and ruin salmon nets. Ultimately, the fishery

decimated these super sharks, described as "common as . . . salmon" in *Basking Sharks: The Slaughter of BC's Gentle Giants*. Unfortunately, Graner's incredible experience with basking sharks in the Salish Sea is a modern anomaly, but perhaps one to be celebrated as a sign that eventually these magnificent sharks will return—not for us to annihilate, but to appreciate and celebrate.

EYE TO EYE WITH THE FISH

Since the invention of the self-contained underwater breathing apparatus (scuba), pioneered by the late Jacques Cousteau, a new group of fish enthusiasts has emerged in the Salish Sea: scuba divers. Although most people cannot contemplate entering the cold, deep waters of the Salish Sea, the region is one of the world's premiere cold-water diving destinations. People brave strong tidal currents and water temperatures in the range of 40° to 50° F (4° to 10°C) to get a glimpse of some of the strangest and most fascinating fish in the world—on the fish's terms. Some of these fish range in size from the 1- to 5-inch (2.5 to 12.7cm) Pacific spiny lumpsucker to the 16-foot (4.9m) bluntnose sixgill shark as well as fish that range in shape from the short and stubby grunt sculpin or the long and snakelike wolf eel to the ornate decorated warbonnet. If you ask 50 scuba divers to name their favorite fish, you are likely to get 50 different answers.

▲ Beyond the size of decorated warbonnets—they can grow to be 16.5 inches (42cm) long—and their markings, distribution, and preferred habitat, not much is known about them. But most concur these eel-shaped fish look both barbaric and whimsical.

The Pacific spiny lumpsucker, or "good little sphere," as the Latin name would suggest, has a ventral sucking disk made from modified pelvic fins that allows the fish to stick to a rock or a piece of eelgrass—an advantage, as this miniballoon of a fish is not much of a swimmer.

◄ Male and female wolf eels den together and guard their eggs until they hatch. Using their powerful jaws, they can crush sea urchins and crabs.

Longfin sculpin are just one of hundreds of beautiful fish species found in the Salish Sea.

Snowy owls are a tundra species that migrates south to spend the winter in the mix of farm fields and tidewater marshes that edge the mainland shores of the Salish Sea. When Arctic lemmings, their preferred food, are in short supply, large numbers of these beautiful and otherworldly owls turn up in places like Vancouver's Boundary Bay Regional Park and Washington's Samish, Padilla, and Skagit Bays, where they can depend on a ready supply of sea ducks, grebes, shorebirds, songbirds, and small mammals.

Now they pass, filling the distance,
a faint flapping of wings against the light,
a throbbing winged unity.

—Pablo Neruda

Epic Journeys

Thousands of migrating western sandpipers, one of the Western Hemisphere's most common shorebirds, lift off the beach in response to a real or imagined threat. Millions of these beautiful sandpipers forage on Salish Sea mudflats en route to coastal breeding sites in western Alaska.

Migration along the Pacific Flyway—the epic journeys that stitch continents together with the feathering of a million wings—leaves an unforgettable vapor trail in the skies above the Salish Sea. This remarkable estuarine ecosystem provides migratory birds with one of the most important energy refueling stops along the entire coastal flyway. Each spring and fall, countless feathered bedouins travel these ancient pathways in the sky, some eddying out to rest and replenish, others pushing relentlessly onward to reach their breeding or overwintering areas, depending on the migratory season.

◀ A single dun-colored female harlequin duck and several brilliantly patterned males brave the surf. No other duck in the region raises its young in a rushing torrent and spends winters in the embrace of storm-tossed seas.

▲ Anna's hummingbirds, year-round residents, brave occasional snow and cold temperatures by visiting artificial nectar feeders and red-breasted sapsucker sap wells in deciduous tree trunks.

▲ A female rufous hummingbird sits on her tiny cup-shaped nest of downy fibers held together by spiderwebs and camouflaged with green moss and lichens. She incubates her 2 eggs, each the size of a coffee bean, for 16 days until they hatch.

When it comes to fueling migratory journeys, birds are evolutionary marvels in their ability to convert food, air, and water into a mileage plan that has no equal in the animal world. The anatomy and "onboard" physiology of a migratory bird is designed to do exactly what that species' life history demands of it—and make it look simple!

Fat is the biofuel of choice for all migrating birds. The source and amount of fat required by each migratory species, however, is unique to that species and may vary seasonally. Fat yields more than twice the energy per ounce (gram) when burned as fuel than either protein or carbohydrate. Fat is also stored "dry" in birds—without the need for supplementary water—so it weighs only one-eighth as much as the stored carbohydrates required to produce the same amount of energy. Furthermore, fat is a "clean-burning" fuel when metabolized by birds, yielding energy, carbon dioxide, and water, without any of the nasty by-products (nitrogenous wastes) that must be excreted from the body.

Eating ravenously appears to be a critical strategy for ensuring migratory success. Prior to departure, as well as at major stopovers—staging areas—en route, migratory birds begin depositing critical fat reserves, eventually shifting from carbohydrate and protein metabolism to primarily burning fat. The longer the flying distance between refueling stopovers, the larger the fat reserves required. Water becomes especially crucial to a bird's ability to combat dehydration during long-distance flight, and the water produced by each ounce (gram) of fat burned can make the difference between life and death. When not actively foraging, migratory birds tend to reduce their energy needs by resting quietly or, in the case of very small birds, like Anna's and rufous hummingbirds, by slipping into an energy-saving state called torpor, which may be sufficient to ensure survival when conditions are harsh.

◀ Mallards, the most common and widespread duck species in North America, overwinter in the marshes, bays, and freshwater wetlands all around the Salish Sea. This group of malachite-green-headed males and brown-plumaged females settled in at a refuge within the heart of the Fraser River estuary.

This single-species cloud of dunlins is a stark contrast to the backdrop of a loading platform for container ships.

SHOREBIRD MAGIC

The majority of long-distance migrants making use of the Salish Sea are shorebirds. The spectacular journeys of these remarkable birds may span South and Central America and cover thousands of miles (km) from their overwintering areas to their preferred breeding sites along the Alaskan coastline and in the high Arctic areas of northeastern Russia and western Canada. At the peak of spring migration, the shores of the Salish Sea, the tidal mudflats, bays, and rocky headlands are alive with shorebirds of every size and shape. At least 2 dozen different species, including western sandpipers, least sandpipers, spotted sandpipers, dunlins, long-billed dowitchers, semipalmated plovers, and black turnstones will touch down, however briefly, to take advantage of the Salish Sea's smorgasbord of invertebrate delicacies.

On the tidal mudflats, the varying lengths and shapes of shorebird bills—long, short, upturned, downturned, straight, or slightly curved—will determine each bird's unique foraging niche. Multiple species can work the food-rich intertidal mudflats side by side and not be in direct competition. The invertebrate bounty of the mudflat includes insects and their larvae, marine worms, tiny crustaceans (shrimp, crabs, and sand fleas), and small mollusks (snails, clams, and mussels). In terms of the sheer biomass of food available, tidal mudflats are among the richest ecosystems in the world.

Semipalmated plovers and western sandpipers rest side by side before continuing their long journey to the Far North tundra and western Alaska.

A bald eagle swoops over an expansive mudflat and a thousand western sandpipers lift off in tight formation, evasively veering left and then right, flashing brown, flashing white, and then settling back down to forage when the threat has passed. For the sparrow-sized sandpiper, the northbound flight is especially perilous; the several-week journey from Peru or Argentina to the western sandpiper's Alaskan breeding sites will take these tiny shorebirds across mountains, deserts, and hundreds of miles of open ocean. Western sandpipers have even been spotted on radar flying at 19,530 feet (5,952.7m)! Biologists believe that the western sandpipers' extra-early migration may be timed so that they get under way ahead of the migrating peregrine falcons that use the same coastal route and relish these sandpipers as hors d'oeuvres on the wing.

Dunlins use their long bills to probe for mollusks, sand fleas, and other crustaceans and marine worms at low tide in the mudflats.

IT "SNOWS" ONLY IN WINTER

In the Skagit Valley, the November weather forecast is always the same—flurries of snow geese. It is estimated that at least 25,000 of the tens of thousands of snow geese that breed on Wrangel Island off the coast of Siberia overwinter on the Fraser River delta, in the Skagit River bottomlands, and at Fir Island, a triangle of fertile farmland fronting Skagit Bay.

The Salish Sea hosts enormous flocks of marine-wintering waterfowl, including canvasbacks, greater scaup, buffleheads, common goldeneyes, and surf scoters. Some species, such as the harlequin duck and the western grebe, will leave marine waters after overwintering and will spend the nesting season along the rivers that run through the Salish Sea's watershed forests. The Salish Sea also provides winter respite for 3 species of wintering loons, including North America's largest congregation of Pacific loons. If you spot a hundred or so of these elegant gray-headed loons rafted up and riding the swells offshore, you will have discovered loon paradise.

▲ Short-eared owls use a close-quartering, tilting to-and-fro manner of flight and their sound-concentrating facial disc as they hunt for prey in open fields and across tidelands.

◄ Huge flocks of overwintering snow geese, members of a subpopulation that breeds on Wrangel Island in the Russian Arctic, are a common but awe-inspiring sight on Washington's Skagit River estuary and British Columbia's Fraser River estuary.

Small numbers of sandhill cranes overwinter at the George C. Reifel Migratory Bird Sanctuary or in the nearby fields of the Fraser River delta in British Columbia. The sight of these elegant waders engaging in a courtship dance and the sound of their unique call as they soar overhead are treats for the senses.

A cloud of migrating shorebirds at sunset adds even more mystery to the thermal and optically induced mirage known as a fata morgana, named for the Arthurian sorceress, Morgan le Fay.

GRAY DAYS AND HUMPBACK NIGHTS

Whales, more than almost any other marine mammal, hold the key to our hearts and our environmental consciousness—theirs is a rallying cry that cannot be denied. In the Salish Sea, the dramatic comeback of 2 champion migrators, the gray whale and the humpback whale, are success stories. Gray whales migrate at least 9,000 miles (14,484km) in eastern Pacific waters during a 12-month period, farther than any other species of whale. The eastern Pacific population overwinters and breeds in the shallow warm water lagoons of Baja California. During their time in Mexican waters, the huge adult gray whales, which reach a maximum length of about 50 feet (15m) and an

average weight of 30 tons (27,216kg), seldom eat, living off the energy stored in their blubber layer. By late winter, they begin traveling north for their annual 5-month Arctic feeding-spree in the Bering, Chukchi, and Beaufort Seas. The gray whale's predictable annual migration route, typically no more than 20 miles (32km) offshore, made them an easy target for commercial whalers, who pushed the species to the brink of extinction by the end of the nineteenth century. Gray whales were finally granted protection in U.S. waters in 1937, with British Columbia following suit, after which the eastern Pacific population rebounded to an estimated 18,000 to 20,000 individuals.

A humpback whale dives, showing its flukes before disappearing into the depths of Rosario Strait.

Aerial Acrobats and Deep Divers

▲ Eagles possess talons that are among the largest and strongest in the bird world, and their ability to catch and carry fish is legendary. This bald eagle, a member of the fish-eagle group, made a talon-first plunge into a school of small forage fish and emerges with a hefty catch.

◄ The pigeon guillemot is the only alcid species that resides in the Salish Sea year-round. In the summer, it is black with a white patch on the wing. In the winter, it is white with a little black on the wing; but year-round, it has red clownlike feet that assist with wing propulsion as it dives.

At the roiling confluence of two tidal currents, the sapphire iridescence of the sea is alive with a raucous feeding frenzy of diving and bobbing seabirds. A pair of bald eagles swoops over the melee like airborne pirates, forcing a few of the fishing birds to drop their catch. You can hear the full measure of the unfolding drama in the cacophony of avian voices. Whether the food of choice is plant or animal, all of the more than 172 bird species associated with the Salish Sea exhibit distinctive adaptations and behaviors that allow them to use the air, the land, and the sea to their advantage. Birds that hunt from the air have aerodynamically designed wings, superb distance vision, precise maneuverability in pursuit of prey, and the ability to fly efficiently and to great heights when traveling over land or water. Those species that exploit food resources in the water are either dedicated divers, magnificently capable of "flying" underwater, or are adapted for effective foraging near the surface or in shallow water. All of these birds must have wing and other anatomical adaptations that suit their water-focused lifestyle and foraging niche as well as a means of waterproofing their feathers.

Ravens are opportunist omnivores in their foraging habits. Working
singly or in pairs, they will sometimes flush nesting seabirds, ducks,
and geese from their nests and then return to seize eggs or young.
This raven's prize is a goose egg.

AERIAL ACROBATS

Soaring aloft is the vision that comes to mind when we think of birds that hunt on the wing. Although bald eagles appear to soar and glide with little effort, their large size and 6-foot (2m) wingspan require optimal flying conditions in order for them to achieve true elegance in flight. Bald eagles have slots on the ends of their wings— fingerlike gaps between the large and primary feathers that help them maintain a steady flight pattern, increase lift, and maneuver precisely. Most people are surprised to learn that as large as eagles are, the hollow-boned skeleton of an eagle weighs less than half as much as the 7,000 or so feathers that cloak its body. High flyers like bald eagles, ravens, and vultures often take advantage of large masses of rising air, called thermals, to effortlessly stay aloft and to reach maximum flight elevation.

Bald eagles are famous for their aerial displays, and this pair, with their talons locked in a spectacular nuptial flight or pair-bonding display, is no exception.

Spending time along the shore or on the water almost guarantees that you'll have the pleasure of watching a bald eagle catch a fish. You may even see the eagle's initial launch from its hunting perch, a sideslip aerial maneuver with the wings slightly folded, which enables it to lose altitude quickly, and then an arrow-straight descent with the legs extended backward and the talons closed like a fist. Once it glides within striking distance, the legs are thrust forward and the talons open to snatch the fish from the water. With the prey secured in its talons, the eagle raises its wings over its back and begins flapping powerfully to regain altitude. A bald eagle's eyesight is legendary, and the expression "eagle eye" refers to the fact that its radarlike visual acuity is 3 to 4 times stronger than ours. The eagle's eyes are extraordinarily large and can be focused both forward and to the side at the same time; excellent color vision allows them to spot their prey in the water from an altitude of 1,000 feet (305m) or more.

Viewing the courtship displays and aerial chases of bald eagles and ravens against the backdrop of the Salish Sea is an unforgettable experience. Bald eagle nuptial flights take airborne choreography to a spectacular level with an array of acrobatic stunts, including cartwheels, roller-coaster swoops, and high-speed chases. If you are truly lucky, you might see a soaring eagle pair drop out of the sky face-to-face, locking their talons together briefly and then unfurling their winged embrace in midair over the water. When it comes to pair-bonding displays, ravens are also wonderful fliers and never disappoint their fans. Male and female ravens often soar together, wheeling and tumbling with seeming abandon, and may be seen flying one above the other with wingtips touching; raven pairs may even pass objects to each other while in flight. Raven vocalizations, ranging from melodious burblings to a deeply resonant *quork, quork, quork*, often provide the musical prelude to these displays.

TAKING THE PLUNGE

Rhinoceros auklets, like other alcids, are ecological counterparts of the Southern Hemisphere penguins. Both groups have short wings when compared to the overall length of the body, which they use to swim underwater in pursuit of prey. The tips of the rhino's wings are comparatively long and pointed, which makes them especially well suited for both swimming and flying fast and close to the surface of the water. The shape of the wings is evident as this rhinoceros auklet has just begun to dive. If the skeleton of the wing were visible, we could see that the humerus is significantly longer than the ulna. Like other alcids, the auklet keeps its feathers waterproofed by the frequent application of "preen" oil from a gland situated above the tail. After an alcid dives and begins to swim underwater, silvery bubbles of air may be seen as they are released from beneath its well-oiled feathers.

DIVERS EXTRAORDINAIRE

▲ Tufted puffins are skilled divers but must use their webbed feet to run across the water to get airborne. They breed on isolated islands in the Strait of Juan de Fuca and the Strait of Georgia where the sediments are soft enough to allow them to excavate burrows or where nesting cavities already exist. Their diet consists mostly of small fish, and they will join auklets and murres at tidal rips that concentrate shoals of forage fish near the surface.

Marine birds live at the mercy of wind and wave—as the sea goes, storm-ridden or serene, so must they. Their survival is inextricably linked to the sea's many moods, its ecological health, and biological productivity. The Salish Sea is home to a diverse assortment of diving birds that "fly" underwater in pursuit of their prey. Water is much like air, only more dense and containing far less oxygen, requiring an entirely different set of adaptations. Members of the alcid family, the Northern Hemisphere's equivalent of penguins, are among the most proficient of Salish Sea divers. These adorable penguinlike seabirds—common murres, pigeon guillemots, marbled and ancient murrelets, Cassin's and rhinoceros auklets, and tufted puffins—come in plumages of black, white, gray, and brown that vary with the season. All have compact bodies, waterproof feathers, legs positioned closer to their tail, and relatively stubby finlike wings that are perfectly suited to underwater flight. Unlike the flightless penguins, alcids strike a fine balance between life in water, in the air, and on land. But like penguins, alcids spend the entire year at sea, coming to shore only to lay their eggs and raise their young. The pigeon guillemot will seek deep crevices in the rocks in which to nest, and the rhinoceros auklet and tufted puffin both prefer to excavate subterranean burrows on remote islands.

◄ The rhinoceros auklet will catch a bill-load of forage fish, like Pacific sand lance, before returning to its burrow to feed its young. How does this bird catch a fish and not lose it when opening its mouth to catch the second or third or even the thirteenth fish? (Yes, some rhinoceros auklets have been documented to hold 13 fish at a time.) Tiny barbs on the bird's bill and tongue keep the fish from getting away when it opens its mouth to catch another.

WHAT'S UP?

Like other sea ducks, the common goldeneye is a strong diver
that stirs up the bottom with its webbed feet to dislodge small prey.
The common goldeneye is a frequent winter resident and migrant
from October to mid-April.

A DIVERSITY OF DIVERS AND A NICHE FOR ALL

Western grebes are perhaps the most aquatic bird in the Salish Sea, never going on land. They winter on the marine waters of the Salish Sea, and in the summer, they breed on freshwater lakes where they build floating nests in emerging aquatic vegetation.

In the Salish Sea, diving birds eat almost every food item imaginable and can be seen foraging in shallow inshore waters and in deeper waters well offshore. Alcids float on the water while resting, propelling themselves about with their webbed feet like ducks, but using their wings to fly underwater when pursuing small fishes, squid, marine worms, and crustaceans. Among the alcids, the dive champions include the common murre, which reaches depths of nearly 600 feet (183m), the rhinoceros auklet, with dives up to just over 200 feet (61m), and the pigeon guillemot, which reaches nearly 100 feet (30m).

Small schooling fish are a diet staple for shallower-diving species, including cormorants, grebes, mergansers, gulls, terns, and belted kingfishers. The surf scoter often takes advantage of herring spawning waters during springtime migration but will focus on diving for clams and mussels at other times of the year. The red-necked phalarope is the only shorebird you are likely to see swimming; most shorebirds are waders or forage on mudflats or the intertidal zone for their food. Like other phalaropes, this species exhibits a distinctive circular swimming behavior, spinning like a top to swirl plankton and other tiny food items to the surface where they can easily be snatched up in the phalarope's beak. Watching belted kingfishers can be a delight; their theatrics are highlighted by high-speed chases, daring headfirst dives, and displays of fishing prowess, all to the sound track of loud chattering flight calls.

Buffleheads are common winter residents and migrants from October to May in the shallow bays and estuaries of the Salish Sea. Courtship displays can be seen in February. This sea duck is a strong diver that feeds on small mollusks, crustaceans, and small fish.

Red-necked phalaropes are plankton eaters and can be found foraging in upwellings or currents. They also create their own upwellings by spinning and kicking, which forces surface water away so rapidly that replacement water fills the void, bringing with it nutritious copepods, euphausiid, and other plankton.

101

A lunge-feeding humpback whale discovers a school of Pacific herring in a tidal rip and attracts a group of opportunist gulls ready to take advantage of the escaping herring.

A BUFFET OR A DOUBLE-DIP?

Small forage fish, such as Pacific herring, surf smelt, Pacific sand lance, northern anchovy, and eulachon, fuel the Salish Sea food web and compensate for their size by forming large, slow-moving, tightly packed schools that offer a concentrated food source for a variety of predators. A rhinoceros auklet swims off with its catch while a glaucous-winged gull observes.

The gray whale . . . despite our history in seeking to destroy it, wants to live closest to us. If they are being forgiving toward us, the implications are enormous.

—Dick Russell

Life in Two Worlds

The story of marine mammals in the Salish Sea is profoundly linked to humans, and as in the past, our interactions with them will continue to affect their existence. Envision a 66,000-pound (29,937kg), 40-foot (12m) humpback whale acrobatically breaching from the water and landing nearby as you sit quietly in a kayak. Close encounters like that make it easy to understand why marine mammals capture the hearts and minds of visitors and residents alike. Of the 38 mammal species known to use the Salish Sea, about 75 percent are marine mammals that completely depend upon the sea and exhibit anatomical and physiological adaptions that enable them to breathe air and live in an undersea world.

◄ Shedding water like a Labrador retriever after a swim, a humpback whale seems to effortlessly launch its 66,000-pound (29,937kg) body as it breaches from the water. Its characteristically large winglike pectoral fins are almost one-third as long as the whale's entire body.

As a Pacific white-sided dolphin prepares to surface, just before its blowhole breaks out of the water, it exhales all the carbon dioxide that has built up during its previous dive and takes in a new breath of air.

As juvenile Steller sea lions get older, they will travel farther from and spend more time away from their haul-out sites. By 1 year of age, they appear to be as capable as adults in their

For the most part, this watery mix of marine mammals comes and goes from the Salish Sea with a complexity of timing and purpose that challenges armchair naturalists and would baffle even parents of multiple teenage drivers. Only one pinniped (the harbor seal) and one cetacean (the harbor porpoise) are local breeders and year-round residents of the Salish Sea. Male Steller and California sea lions are routinely seen, but generally leave for the summer when they travel to rookeries on the outer coast to breed. Elephant seals, on the other hand, breed during the winter in Mexico and California, but can be sighted year-round in the Salish Sea. Odontocetes (toothed whales, including Dall's porpoise, Pacific white-sided dolphins, and killer whales) and mysticetes (baleen whales, like humpbacks, grays, and minkes) can be seen year-round, but will leave to visit other feeding locations or, in

GRAY WHALES AND SCOTERS: STRANGE TABLEMATES

Gray whales excel at rummaging in the muddy seafloor for tiny amphipods, marine worms, and ghost shrimp, a unique feeding niche that apparently minimizes competition with other whale species. Using their 2,500-pound (1,134kg) tongue as a retractable suction device and the baleen in the upper jaw as a filter, gray whales "hose in" about 67 tons (60,781kg) of small mud-dwelling invertebrates during their spring-summer foraging extravaganza. As they forage, gray whales create elliptical suction pits that can be 4 inches (10cm) deep and cover an area of up to 53 square feet (5sq. m). Whales are not the sole beneficiaries of this behavior. The pits expose or dislodge invertebrates in the mud, making food available for other species, including some that are imperiled. Gray whales provide scoters—sea ducks that have shown a precipitous population decline in the Salish Sea over the past few decades—with food resources just when their nutritional requirements are high as they prepare for migration and reproduction. Do gray whales know they are helping scoters? Probably not, but the symbolism of a recovered whale "helping" a species at risk is worth celebrating.

THE ART OF LIVING UNDERWATER

Marine mammals, as well as many diving seabirds and sea ducks, possess an astonishing ability to conduct most aspects of their lives underwater, even though they breathe air. But exactly how do air-breathing animals hold their breath for long periods of time as they travel, avoid predators, search for food—and in the case of whales, communicate?

Obviously, the first step an animal takes as it dives is to do what we do: stop breathing. But how are they able to stay underwater for so much longer than we can? When they dive, they are no longer taking in air to oxygenate their blood, so they slow their heart rate and even reduce or stop the flow of blood to nonessential organs (for example, skin or stomach) and preferentially send the blood to more important sites, such as the heart and brain.

As the diving animal moves about underwater, huge amounts of myoglobin (an oxygen-storing molecule in the muscle that works as hemoglobin does in the blood) provide oxygen to the working muscles. In addition, diving birds and mammals can tolerate very high levels of carbon dioxide (CO_2), the molecule that creates the urge to breathe. As they come to the surface, they exhale all that CO_2, take a breath, replenish their muscle myoglobin with oxygen, and get ready to dive again.

Juvenile Steller sea lions are delightfully entertaining, but adult males can weigh up to 2,400 pounds (1,088kg), 3 times the size of an adult male grizzly bear. Fortunately, most scuba divers report being ignored by big bulls or, in worst cases, a sea lion will gently tug at a diver's flipper or ankle as if to say *You're not welcome here.* Grizzly bears wouldn't be so kind.

THE ELITE—DIVING DEEP

Deep dives are more difficult than shallow dives for birds and mammals not only because they are required to hold their breath for longer periods but also because they have to deal with increasing water pressure at increased depths. Remember: For every 33 feet (10m) or so below the surface, pressure increases by 1 atmosphere (14.7psi). Many animals are able to deal with high pressure at depth because they have flexible bodies that can withstand the pressure and they are able to circulate their blood through protected sinuses to other organs (the brain, for example). Our bodies would be crushed at a depth of 1 mile (1.6km), whereas an elephant seal at the same depth is not only comfortable but able to catch food.

You might think that larger birds and mammals can dive deeper than smaller ones. But that is not always true. Baleen whales are not very deep divers when you consider their size. If dive depth is compared to body size, the Salish Sea seals (for example, harbor seals and elephant seals) and alcids (like common murres and rhinoceros auklets) are the best divers, hands down.

Pacific white-sided dolphins and Dall's porpoise are not afraid of boats and will even commonly surf at the bow or stern of passing vessels. The smaller harbor porpoise, however, tends to be shy and sedate, rarely riding a boat's bow or showing much more than a dorsal fin. Harbor porpoise will occasionally mate with Dall's porpoise.

HOW DEEP CAN THEY DIVE?

COMMON NAME	MAXIMUM DIVING DEPTH (IN FEET AND METERS)
Mink	9.7 (3.0m)
Surf scoter	39.4 (12.0m)
Marbled murrelet	44.9 (13.7m)
North American river otter	98.4 (30.0m)
Pigeon guillemot	98.4 (30.0m)
Human (scuba diver)	120.0 (36.6m)
Long-tailed duck	200.1 (61.0m)
Common loon	200.1 (61.0m)
Rhinoceros auklet	213.3 (65.0m)
Sea otter	318.0 (96.9m)
Humpback whale	485.6 (148.0m)
Gray whale	555.7 (169.4m)
Common murre	590.6 (180.0m)
Dall's porpoise	590.6 (180.0m)
Pacific white-sided dolphin	702.1 (214.0m)
Harbor porpoise	741.5 (226.0m)
Killer whale	1397.6 (426.0m)
Harbor seal	1666.7 (508.0m)
Leatherback sea turtle	4265.1 (1300.0m)
Northern elephant seal	5692.3 (1735.0m)

IDENTIFYING KILLER WHALES

This killer whale looks as if it has a unique tattoo on its neck, although the "marking" is actually the shadow of a gull. But wouldn't it be great if all killer whales could be identified by their specific markings? Fortunately, they can. In 1974, Michael Bigg, a scientist with the Canadian Department of Fisheries and Oceans, followed by Ken Balcomb, with the Center for Whale Research, and other scientists, photographed thousands of killer whales, and after examining the images, they realized that each whale could be identified by the shape of its dorsal fin and the pigmentation pattern of its saddle patch at the base of its dorsal fin. The ability to identify every killer whale in the Salish Sea has benefitted our understanding of killer whale ecotypes, behavior, and longevity and has helped us to realize the impact of toxins and diseases on the long-term survival of these animals.

ARE KILLER WHALES REALLY "KILLERS OF WHALES"?

Yes and no. Some will kill and eat other whales—a behavior noted by early whalers who created the epithet. We now know, however, that not all killer whales have this dietary preference. In some parts of the world, there are killer whale subtypes, or ecotypes, that specialize in certain prey. The Salish Sea is home to 3 distinct killer whale ecotypes. Residents are the most well-known ecotype, and these whales prefer fish, specifically salmon. The marine mammal eaters are called transients. Members of the third and less well-known ecotype, offshores, are believed to be fish specialists that appear to have a preference for eating sharks.

Scientists have shown that the better-known resident and transient killer whales not only prefer different diets but also have genetic, behavioral, vocal, and morphologic differences. The offshore ecotype, which has not been studied as intensively, is genetically distinct from the resident and transient ecotypes, although it is more closely related to residents than transients. Ecological specialization—with accompanying social and reproductive isolation of offshore, resident, and transient killer whale ecotypes—has led to a divergence and one day might even lead to their classification as distinct subspecies or species.

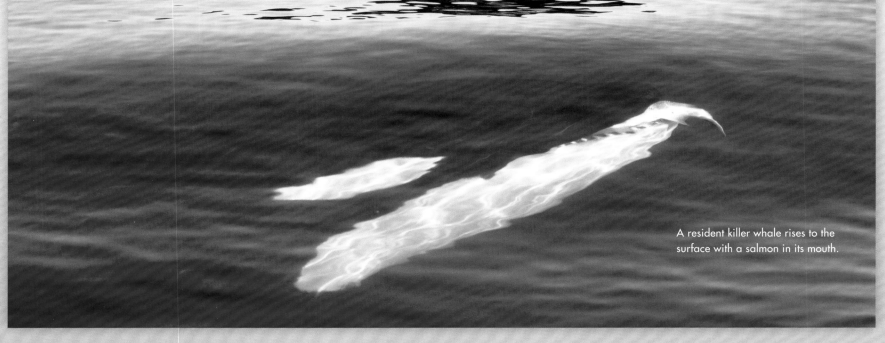

A resident killer whale rises to the surface with a salmon in its mouth.

URBAN WHALES: "SPEAKING" LOUDER AND LONGER

Killer whales and other toothed whales are guided by sound in all aspects of their lives. They use sound to communicate, locate food, and navigate an undersea world often limited by visibility. To echolocate, they produce sound by moving air across two vibratory structures called phonic lips, located inside their blowhole. The sound is then directed through the fatty melon in the whale's forehead and directed out toward objects in the water. Returning sound waves are carried to the ear by the lower jaw and associated fat and air spaces. Loud underwater noises—like those from a ship—can significantly reduce a whale's ability to communicate or locate prey. Scientists have discovered an interesting reaction among killer whales subjected to high levels of noise underwater. Apparently, they behave as we do at a loud rock concert: They "speak" louder and hold each syllable longer, increasing the amplitude and duration of their call.

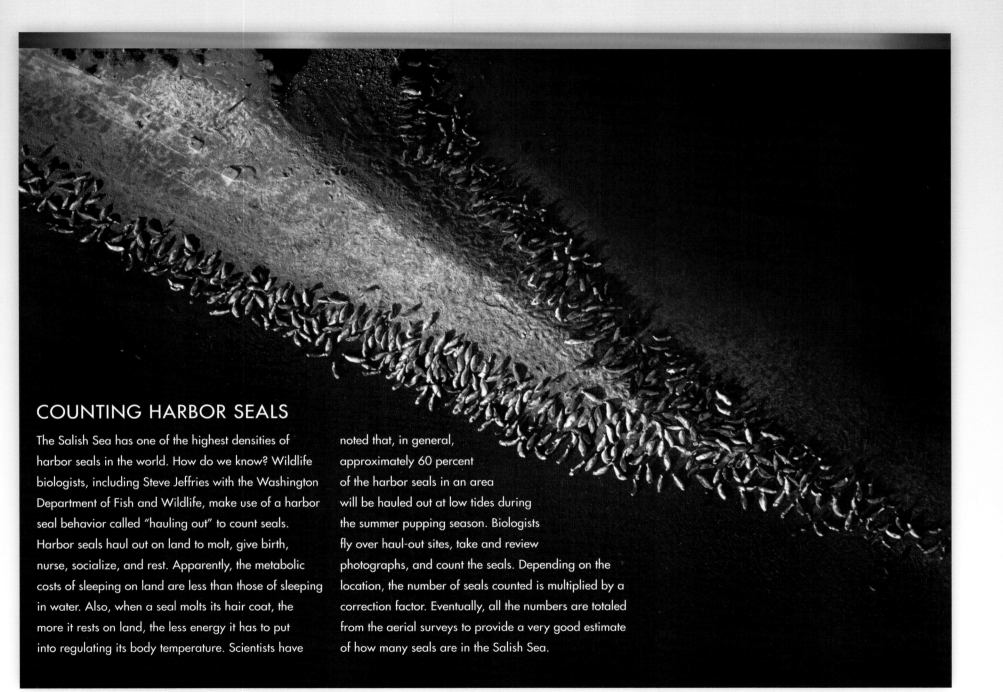

COUNTING HARBOR SEALS

The Salish Sea has one of the highest densities of harbor seals in the world. How do we know? Wildlife biologists, including Steve Jeffries with the Washington Department of Fish and Wildlife, make use of a harbor seal behavior called "hauling out" to count seals. Harbor seals haul out on land to molt, give birth, nurse, socialize, and rest. Apparently, the metabolic costs of sleeping on land are less than those of sleeping in water. Also, when a seal molts its hair coat, the more it rests on land, the less energy it has to put into regulating its body temperature. Scientists have noted that, in general, approximately 60 percent of the harbor seals in an area will be hauled out at low tides during the summer pupping season. Biologists fly over haul-out sites, take and review photographs, and count the seals. Depending on the location, the number of seals counted is multiplied by a correction factor. Eventually, all the numbers are totaled from the aerial surveys to provide a very good estimate of how many seals are in the Salish Sea.

The more we know of other forms of life,

the more we enjoy and respect ourselves. . . .

Humanity is exalted not because we are so far above

other living creatures but because knowing them well

elevates the very concept of life.

—E. O. Wilson

Tidelines and Lifeways

◄ Coast Salish women considered young red cedars, no more than 2 hand spans wide, the best size from which to harvest the cedar's inner bark. Sufficient bark is always left on the tree to ensure unimpeded sap flow to the root system and continued tree growth.

The Coast Salish have lived along the shores of the Salish Sea since the Pleistocene glaciers retreated north and the land and sea were emerging anew. Their lifeways and cultural traditions did and still do reflect an intimate relationship with the natural world—a sense of place intertwined with the sea and the forests that embrace its shores. Salish Sea waters once teemed with salmon, and tidal flats were replete with shellfish, a seemingly infinite plenitude that supported an extraordinarily vibrant culture. Red cedar—the Coast Salish tree of life—was woven into the fabric of daily life. For the Coast Salish people, the abundant resources of land and sea, unparalleled elsewhere in North America, offered the stability to build a rich culture and a lifeway that honored sustainability.

In a ceremonial gathering of canoes, Tsleil-Waututh, Squamish, Musqueam, and other First Nations protest against the expansion of a crude-oil pipeline and construction of a new marine shipping terminal that endanger natural resources critical to their culture and well-being.

Coast Salish women harvested the cedar's flexible branchlets (the withes) and its fibrous inner bark and used these materials to create a wide array of utilitarian and decorative items for everyday living. The method for preparing the bark remains much the same today as in the past. The harvester makes a horizontal cut across the tree's "belly" (the side with the fewest branches) and then pries up a strip of bark so that it can be pulled free by walking backward. The bark is then pounded and shredded into thin flexible strips that can be twined, plaited, and woven to make rope, fishing nets, mats, baskets, hats, and other garments.

Coast Salish men used the straight-grained and supremely rot-resistant wood for building homes and for carving totems and other ceremonial items, and they turned the massive trunks into seaworthy dugout canoes. These remarkable canoes, usually made from a single huge log expertly hollowed out and shaped using the simplest of tools, were much admired by the first Europeans to reach the shores of the Salish Sea. Nowhere else in the world were dugout canoes built that could match these for speed, capacity, beauty, or seaworthiness. Coast Salish are still building and using these canoes today.

Edward Sheriff Curtis (ca. 1912)

A female killer whale, identified by her dorsal fin and saddle patch as L47, travels past Elliot Bay and Seattle's waterfront, reminding us that we share the Salish Sea ecosystem with the wildlife we love and admire—and that the future of these creatures is profoundly affected by our actions.

QUALITY OF LIFE

There is tremendous beauty in the ways that the Salish Sea and human lifeways have evolved over time. The extraordinary quality of life enjoyed here, one that depends on a healthy Salish Sea, cannot be replicated elsewhere. Imagine, for a moment, sailing along one of the Salish Sea's designated marine highways. As you look toward the mainland, towering volcanoes and snowcapped mountains provide an idyllic backdrop for homes and communities and for commercial and recreational activities. On a typical summer day, passenger and auto ferries pass to and fro; container ships steam toward the major port cities of Seattle, Tacoma, or Vancouver; cruise ships head for the waters of British Columbia and Alaska; tugboats tow huge rafts of logs; and a flurry of fishing and crabbing boats set out for the day. On quieter waters, residents and visitors enjoy world-class recreational opportunities, including sea kayaking, kite surfing, boating, fishing, scuba diving, and whale watching. The billions of dollars generated by Salish Sea–based commercial and recreational activities fuel an exceptionally strong economy on both sides of the international border.

Workers assembling a log boom share the waves with surfers and kayakers at the mouth of the Jordan River, Strait of Juan de Fuca, British Columbia.

A diver admires giant plumose anemones, reported to be the world's tallest
anemone, reaching heights of 3 feet (1m).

A scuba diver and a wolf eel enjoy a close and mutually curious encounter.

A lone sea kayaker paddles into the sunset at Deception Pass.
The numerous islands, complex shorelines, and amazing wildlife make
the Salish Sea a mecca for sea kayakers.

REEF NETTING FOR SOCKEYE

*Those who learn to listen to the world
that sustains them can hear the message
brought forth by the salmon.*

—Billy Frank, Jr. (1931–2014),
Nisqually statesman and activist

Reef-net fishing, an ancient Coast Salish method, was practiced for centuries. Using cedar canoes, platforms, and nets made of cedar, men used a novel method called reef netting to catch sockeye and other wild salmon species. Today, Coast Salish tribes as well as small non-native commercial fisheries, like Lummi Island Wild, have reinvigorated reef netting as an eco-friendly and bycatch-free method of delivering high-quality salmon to consumers. The new reef-net method is fundamentally unchanged from the traditional one except that the boats are slightly bigger and winches are used to retrieve a nylon net. Imagine a reef-netting crew setting up its gear to take advantage of the flood tide when the spawning sockeye are heading to the Fraser River. Designed to mimic a natural underwater reef, two boats are anchored to the bottom of a rocky channel and ribbons of kelp dangle from lines, effectively forming a gauntlet between the boats. The fish are compelled to swim between the boats and into a hammock-like net while observers stand on high towers mounted on the boats and alert the net handlers when to retrieve the nets. The fish are handled with utmost care and quickly sorted; any unwanted species are diverted back into the water. No fossil fuels are expended chasing the salmon; there is virtually no bycatch and very little disruption to marine mammals or birds. Reef-net fishing is just one example of the many ways that seafood providers are striving for a sustainable balance between harvesting the sea's resources, making a good living, and maintaining the health of the Salish Sea for ourselves and for future generations.

The crew of Lummi Island Wild brings in the catch.

A SUSTAINABLE FUTURE

One simple truth guides our stewardship of the Salish Sea: The more biologically diverse and healthy the natural world is, the better it will adapt to change and the greater will be its ability to take care of us. By distilling the magical essence of the Salish Sea, we have portrayed the many ways that the sea and its watersheds are part of an interconnected web of life like no other on Earth. People are a critical part of that web of life. And we do belong here. We, non-native immigrants and Coast Salish tribal members alike, are all citizens of a vibrant Salish Sea community that depends on a resilient partnership between the land, sea, and people. The modern world is in fast-forward mode, and the exponential population growth on both sides of the international border forces us to constantly fine-tune our "business as usual" relationship with the sea. When region-wide toxic pollution levels made international news in the 1980s, scientists, governmental agencies, and citizen activists on both sides of the border began working together to heal the Salish Sea. It didn't take long to see that some affected marine habitats required restoration and recovery if they were to support viable populations of marine animals once again.

All who fish for salmon commercially or recreationally and those who love to eat salmon understand these beautiful fish are as essential to the health and well-being of the Salish Sea as the air we breathe. In contrast to the Atlantic salmon, sockeye have never been farmed or successfully reared in hatcheries for later release into the wild. These spawning sockeye salmon have congregated in the narrows on their way to their Fraser River natal waters.

Geoducks, the world's largest burrowing clams, grow rapidly with most reaching 1.5 pounds (0.7kg) in 3 to 5 years, although some can grow to more than 8 pounds (3.6kg) and live to be over 150 years old. Yes, they look rather strange, but they are delicious!

The smooth pink scallop, one of the most beautiful and delicious of all scallops, is the only one cooked and served in its shell. These swimming bivalves move in the current, flapping their shells like castanets to bring in the plankton they eat. Among the bivalves, scallops alone possess eyes, but they see only shadows out of the dozens of dot-like eyes that ring the filmy skirt-like mantle that drapes the outer edge of the shell. Each eye has a lens, retina, cornea, and optic nerve. Normally, the pink scallop is distinguished by a species of encrusting sponge that cloaks the upper shell, providing the scallop with tactile camouflage that repels, on contact, the scallop's arch predator, the sea star. These scallops are a rare delicacy, harvested sustainably by divers who swim along the rocky reef habitats that the scallops prefer, removing them by hand and transferring them to a mesh bucket.

Many of the people who make a living by providing the seafood we love to eat know what is at stake if we fail to act when the health of the Salish Sea is threatened. They are at the forefront of a more sustainable fishery, whether it has fins or a shell. Shellfish—clams, mussels, oysters, and scallops, for example—are filter feeders and play an important role in filtering and cleaning the waters of the Salish Sea. In performing this service, they also become canaries in the coal mine. By regularly monitoring shellfish, investigators are able to see where contaminant levels are high or where runoff from the land is polluting the ocean with human fecal bacteria or chemicals that pose a health risk to consumers. Shellfish growers, people caring for community shellfish farms, and wild shellfish harvesters are then able to spearhead local recovery efforts that improve water quality, benefit shellfish harvest, and improve the ecosystem for the thousands of other species that depend on clean water.

▲ For the Taylor family, it began in the 1890s when a great-grandfather started farming Olympia oysters in the pristine waters of Puget Sound. Five generations later, Taylor Shellfish Farms has become the largest producer of farmed shellfish in the United States, with 11,000 acres (4,452ha) of tidelands in production. The family business is committed to using sustainable aquaculture practices that emphasize healthy watersheds, healthy estuaries, and healthy communities. A Taylor Shellfish Farms aquaculture specialist inspects a longline system used for culturing clams.

A plate of raw oysters on the half shell exemplifies the definition of ecosystem goods: good to eat, good for the economy, and good for improving water quality.

Killer whales passing by the Turn Point Lighthouse on Stuart Island against the backdrop of Mount Baker remind us all that the Salish Sea improves the quality of life for residents and visitors in ways that cannot always be calculated.

Ask residents of the Salish Sea region if being a part of this ecosystem improves their quality of life, and you will hear that it does. Some might struggle to tell you exactly how their lives are improved, while others are eloquent: They love the view from their waterfront home; they live to go fishing with their kids on the weekend; they love to buy fresh-caught salmon from the market; or they enjoy the salty fragrance of the sea that perfumes the beach during a low summer tide. Economists are challenged to quantify these very personal experiences, but clearly they are as important to the local economy as they are to the people who live here. Whether you depend on the sea for your living or indirectly for your quality of life, we all benefit from a healthy Salish Sea and we all have an obligation to care for it.

A family explores the beach at Golden Gardens Park in Seattle, Washington.

◄ Large tracts of land that used to be flooded intermittently by rivers have been completely altered. The land has been turned into productive farms or towns, but it no longer supports the diversity and abundance of fish and wildlife it once did.

For us Indian people,
all of western Washington was once a food forest.
The trouble is that it's getting harder and harder
for these forests, rivers and beaches
to provide us with much food
because they've been treated so poorly.

—Billy Frank, Jr., "Being Frank," *Northwest Indian Fisheries Commission News,* August 5, 2013

Finding Hope in a Cautionary Tale

If healthy ecosystems foster economic prosperity, unhealthy ones represent lost opportunity and income. The Salish Sea is an ecological jewel, but to be completely honest, we could have done a much better job of taking care of it. Over the past 200 years, humans have drastically altered the Salish Sea to a degree previously associated only with the geological creation of ecosystems. As a result, we have diminished the ecosystem's ability to provide for us.

The number of salmon that return to their natal streams to spawn is now a mere fraction of what it once was, and nobody is "walking across the stream on the backs of salmon." Populations of other culturally important species, like northern abalone, are so depleted that they can no longer be harvested. Cedar trees substantial enough to be used by Coast Salish to make extraordinary seagoing dugout canoes with wide beams and sweeping bows are now so rare that tribes or First Nations wanting to make a canoe must work harder to find a tree than to make the magnificent work of art. Man-made contaminants have infiltrated fish and wildlife populations to levels where they are not only causing health problems in fish, shellfish, and birds, but also putting humans who consume them at risk. And in some areas, human development has altered or completely eliminated critical habitats from the Salish Sea. The construction of river levees, for example, has entirely destroyed floodplains, deltas, and salt marshes.

Unfortunately, looming threats like climate change and ocean acidification are not going to make it easy for us to make amends for what has been done. In certain watersheds, the changing climate is predicted to increase winter river flows and flooding while decreasing summer flows, which will further threaten salmon and steelhead. Ocean acidification—the progressive increase in the acidity of the ocean over an extended period primarily because of uptake of carbon dioxide from the atmosphere—will impact the survival and growth of larvae for culturally, ecologically, and economically important species, including oysters, clams, and mussels, and likely pteropods, red sea urchins, and northern abalone as well. When we consider, in addition, projections for population growth in the region, the picture for the Salish Sea is not rosy.

As our view of what is "normal" is shifted by environmental effects, we will have to adjust our vocabulary as well. We might mistakenly call a cedar tree *big* because we have forgotten how big cedar trees used to be.

◄ Cities, like Vancouver, that surround the Salish Sea are defined not so much by their skyline but by the inland sea that laps at their shores, creates million-dollar views, and provides the wildlife that nurtures the bellies and the souls of their inhabitants. We are the Salish Sea.

RECONCILING COMPETING INTERESTS

The Salish Sea, called by some the gateway to the Pacific Rim, is important for moving forest products, coal, oil, and manufactured materials from North America to the far corners of the Pacific. The economic benefits of this trade could be substantial. At the same time, there are significant negative impacts from shipping like increased underwater noise and increased risk of oil spills that threaten local marine resources. Citizens of the Salish Sea have to decide how to balance competing interests.

The harvest of herring presents a similar quandary. The herring industry provides jobs, delicious local food, and even bait for the recreational salmon fishing industry. Herring also feed wild salmon, lingcod, seabirds, sea ducks, minke whales, humpback whales, and an assortment of other marine wildlife species. The abundance of herring predators is good for recreational fishing and watchable wildlife—two industries that provide jobs and redistribute wealth around the region. How do we balance the desire of the herring industry to promote jobs and provide food for the human population and bait for recreational fishing with the needs of the ecosystem? Balancing competing interests is never simple, but scientists are working with economists, policy makers, and local citizens to improve the decision-making process.

So what do we do? Or as Martha Kongsgaard, chair of the Puget Sound Partnership's Leadership Council and one of the region's thought leaders on Salish Sea recovery, asked: "If nature is humanity's landlord, and we have been getting a rockin' great deal on rent and utilities on both sides of the border and business as usual might be a thing of the past, now what?" The first step in saving a place, or as scientists call it, place-based conservation, is for people to know their ecosystem.

Proposals to expand or build new marine terminals for shipping coal, crude oil, and consumer goods represent the challenges faced when balancing growth and increasing commerce with the ecological well-being of the Salish Sea.

That means the more than 8 million human residents of the Salish Sea need not only to be able to define the boundaries of the ecosystem but also to understand how it was created, to know its history, and to be able to identify the parts and processes necessary to make it work. Once people know a place—and that includes knowing seemingly trivial highly detailed facts about it (for example, that the female giant Pacific octopus has 2,240 suckers)—they become connected to it. And once people connect to an ecosystem, it becomes personal and they want to protect and restore it. Know, connect, protect, and restore. Simple, but not a new thought. Rachel Carson wrote, "The more clearly we can focus our attention on the wonders and realities of the universe about us, the less taste we shall have for destruction."

Dwarfed by the 6-foot (2m) dorsal fin of a passing male killer whale, bystanders gaze in awe.

The people of the Salish Sea have rapidly embraced this ecosystem, which was only recently named. Once commonly used names like Puget Sound, Strait of Juan de Fuca, San Juan Islands, Gulf Islands, and Strait of Georgia are slipping from the vocabulary in favor of the more encompassing name: the Salish Sea. Canadian and U.S. provincial, state, and federal agencies are looking for ways to work together, taking cues from the earliest inhabitants of the region—the people of the Coast Salish tribes and First Nations—who never knew a border. Among the 8 million who reside in the region today, many are thinking ecosystem. World-class aquariums in Seattle and Vancouver and hundreds of other nonprofit marine education groups are helping people know this jewel of the Pacific Northwest and inspiring them not only to care but to take action. Scientists are studying almost every major aspect of the ecosystem, and governmental and nongovernmental groups are restoring numerous aspects of the landscape, from small streams and sections of shoreline to entire river deltas. A sea change is upon the Salish Sea, and it is time for all of us to get on that wave and ride like we stole it.

In our dream for the Salish Sea, we see a day when we all recognize and know our marine resources better than we now know corporate logos. We will watch and monitor the ecosystem better than we now watch the weather or monitor the NASDAQ or Dow Jones Industrial Average. And we will restore and protect the Salish Sea as if our lives and our livelihoods depend on it—because they do.

◀ From streams and rivers to the depths of the ocean where light does not even penetrate, scientists are working to better understand the Salish Sea and provide information that will help managers, policy makers, and local citizens make decisions that consider the long-term health of the Salish Sea.

Appendices

SPECIES LISTS

INVERTEBRATES (IN TEXT)

acorn barnacle *(Balanus glandula)* • brooding anemone *(Epiactis prolifera)* • California sea cucumber *(Parastichopus californicus)*; candy stripe shrimp *(Lebbeus grandimanus)*; cloud sponge *(Aphrocallistes vastus)*; clown nudibranch *(Triopha catalinae)*; Cockerell's nudibranch *(Laila cockerelli)*; crimson anemone *(Cribrinopsis fernaldi)* • daisy brittle star *(Ophiopholis aculeate)* • egg-yolk jelly *(Phacellophora camtschatica)* • geoduck *(Panopea abrupta)*; giant barnacle *(Balanus nubilus)*; giant Pacific octopus *(Octopus dofleini)*; goose neck barnacle *(Mitella polymerus)*; gumboot chiton *(Cryptochiton stelleri)* • hooded nudibranch *(Melibe leonine)* • jeweled top snail *(Calliostoma annulatum)* • leather sea star *(Dermasterias imbricata)* • market squid *(Loligo opalescens)* • northern abalone *(Haliotis kamtschatkana)*; northern kelp crab *(Pugettia producta)* • ochre sea star *(Pisaster ochraceus)*; opalescent nudibranch *(Hermissenda crassicornis)*; orange cup coral *(Balanophyllia elegans)*; orange hermit crab *(Elassochirus gilli)*; orange sea cucumber *(Cucumaria miniata)*; orange sea pen *(Ptilosarcus gurneyi)* • painted anemone *(Urticina crassicornis)*; pink-tipped anemone *(Anthopleura elegantissima)*; plumose anemone *(Metridium giganteum)*; predaceous aeolis *(Flabellina trophina)*; Puget Sound king crab *(Lopholithodes mandtii)*; purple shore crab *(Hemigrapsus nudus)* • red sea urchin *(Strongylocentrotus franciscanus)* • sea lemon *(Archidoris montereyensis)*; skeleton shrimp *(Caprella angusta)*; Snyder blade shrimp *(Spirontocaris snyderi)*; strawberry anemone *(Corynactis californica)*; stubby squid *(Rossia pacifica)*; swimming anemone *(Stomphia didemon)* • white-spotted anemone *(Urticina lofotensis)*

FISH OF THE SALISH SEA

American shad *(Alosa sapidissima)*; arrow goby *(Clevelandia ios)*; arrowtooth flounder *(Atheresthes stomias)*; Atlantic salmon *(Salmo salar)* • basking shark *(Cetorhinus maximus)*; bay goby *(Lepidogobius lepidus)*; bay pipefish *(Syngnathus leptorhynchus)*; Bering eelpout *(Lycodes beringi)*; Bering skate *(Bathyraja interrupta)*; big skate *(Raja binoculata)*; bigeye poacher *(Bathyagonus pentacanthus)*; bigfin eelpout *(Lycodes cortezianus)*; black prickleback *(Xiphister atropurpureus)*; black rockfish *(Sebastes melanops)*; blackbelly eelpout *(Lycodes pacificus)*; blackeye goby *(Rhinogobiops nicholsii)*; blackfin poacher *(Bathyagonus nigripinnis)*; blackfin sculpin *(Malacocottus kincaidi)*; blacktail snailfish *(Careproctus melanurus)*; blacktip poacher *(Xeneretmus latifrons)*; blue lanternfish *(Tarletonbeania crenularis)*; blue rockfish *(Sebastes mystinus)*; blue shark *(Prionace glauca)*; bluebarred prickleback *(Plectobranchus evides)*; bluespotted poacher *(Xeneretmus triacanthus)*; bluntnose sixgill shark *(Hexanchus griseus)*; bocaccio *(Sebastes paucispinis)*; bonehead sculpin *(Artedius notospilotus;* broadnose sevengill shark *(Notorynchus cepedianus)*; brown cat shark *(Apristurus brunneus)*; brown Irish lord *(Hemilepidotus spinosus)*; brown rockfish *(Sebastes auriculatus)*; buffalo sculpin *(Enophrys bison)*; bull trout *(Salvelinus confluentus)*; butter sole *(Isopsetta isolepis)* • C-O sole *(Pleuronichthys coenosus)*; cabezon *(Scorpaenichthys marmoratus)*; calico sculpin *(Clinocottus embryum)*; California flashlightfish *(Protomyctophum crockery)*; California headlightfish *(Diaphus theta)*; California lizardfish *(Synodus lucioceps)*; California skate *(Raja inornata)*; California tonguefish *(Symphurus atricaudus)*; canary rockfish *(Sebastes pinniger)*; capelin *(Mallotus villosus)*; China rockfish *(Sebastes nebulosus)*; chinook salmon *(Oncorhynchus tshawytscha)*; chum salmon *(Oncorhynchus keta)*; coastrange sculpin *(Cottus aleuticus)*; coho salmon *(Oncorhynchus kisutch)*; common carp *(Cyprinus carpio)*;

copper rockfish *(Sebastes caurinus)*; crescent gunnel *(Pholis laeta)*; curlfin sole *(Pleuronichthys decurrens)*; cutthroat trout *(Oncorhynchus clarkii)* • darkblotched rockfish *(Sebastes crameri)*; darter sculpin *(Radulinus boleoides)*; daubed shanny *(Leptoclinus maculatus)*; decorated warbonnet *(Chirolophis decorates)*; dolly varden *(Salvelinus malma)*; Dover sole *(Microstomus pacificus)*; dusky sculpin *(Icelinus burchami)*; dwarf wrymouth *(Cryptacanthodes aleutensis)* • English sole *(Parophrys vetulus)*; eulachon *(Thaleichthys pacificus)* • flathead sole *(Hippoglossoides elassodon*; fluffy sculpin *(Oligocottus snyderi)*; fourhorn poacher *(Hypsagonus quadricornis)*; fringed sculpin *(Icelinus fimbriatus)* • giant wrymouth *(Cryptacanthodes giganteus)*; graveldiver *(Scytalina cerdale)*; gray starsnout *(Bathyagonus alascanus)*; great sculpin *(Myoxocephalus polyacanthocephalus)*; green sturgeon *(Acipenser medirostris)*; greenstriped rockfish *(Sebastes elongates)*; grunt sculpin *(Rhamphocottus richardsonii)* • halfbanded rockfish *(Sebastes semicinctus)*; high cockscomb *(Anoplarchus purpurescens)*; hybrid sole *(Inopsetta ischyra)* • jack mackerel *(Trachurus symmetricus)* • kelp greenling *(Hexagrammos decagrammus)*; kelp perch *(Brachyistius frenatus)*; king-of-the-salmon *(Trachipterus altivelis)* • leopard shark *(Triakis semifasciata)*; lingcod *(Ophiodon elongatus)*; lobefin snailfish *(Liparis greeni)*; longfin gunnel *(Pholis clemensi)*; longfin sculpin *(Jordania zonope)*; longfin smelt *(Spirinchus thaleichthys)*; longnose lancetfish *(Alepisaurus ferox)*; longnose skate *(Raja rhina)*; longsnout prickleback *(Lumpenella longirostris)*; longspine combfish *(Zaniolepis latipinnis)*; lowcrest hatchetfish *(Argyropelecus sladeni)* • manacled sculpin *(Synchirus gilli)*; marbled snailfish *(Liparis dennyi)*; mosshead sculpin *(Clinocottus globiceps)*; mosshead warbonnet *(Chirolophis nugator)* • night smelt *(Spirinchus starksi)*; north Pacific frostfish *(Benthodesmus pacificus)*; northern anchovy *(Engraulis mordax)*; northern clingfish *(Gobiesox maeandricus)*; northern flashlightfish *(Protomyctophum thompsoni)*; northern lampfish *(Stenobrachius leucopsarus)*; northern rock sole *(Lepidopsetta polyxystra)*; northern

ronquil *(Ronquilus jordani)*; northern sculpin *(Icelinus borealis)*; northern smoothtongue *(Leuroglossus schmidti)*; northern spearnose poacher *(Agonopsis vulsa)* • ocean sunfish *(Mola mola)*; opah *(Lampris guttatus)* • Pacific angel shark *(Squatina californica)*; Pacific barracuda *(Sphyraena argentea*; Pacific bonito *(Sarda chiliensis)*; Pacific chub mackerel *(Scomber japonicus)*; Pacific cod *(Gadus macrocephalus)*; Pacific electric ray *(Torpedo californica)*; Pacific hagfish *(Eptatretus stoutii)*; Pacific hake *(Merluccius productus)*; Pacific halibut *(Hippoglossus stenolepis)*; Pacific herring *(Clupea pallasii)*; Pacific lamprey *(Entosphenus tridentatus)*; Pacific ocean perch *(Sebastes alutus)*; Pacific pomfret *(Brama japonica)*; Pacific pompano *(Peprilus simillimus)*; Pacific sand lance *(Ammodytes personatus)*; Pacific sanddab *(Citharichthys sordidus)*; Pacific sandfish *(Trichodon trichodon)*; Pacific sardine *(Sardinops sagax)*; Pacific saury *(Cololabis saira)*; Pacific sleeper shark *(Somniosus pacificus)*; Pacific spiny lumpsucker *(Eumicrotremus orbis)*; Pacific staghorn sculpin *(Leptocottus armatus)*; Pacific tomcod *(Microgadus proximus)*; Pacific viperfish *(Chauliodus macouni)*; padded sculpin *(Artedius fenestralis)*; painted greenling *(Oxylebius pictus)*; pallid eelpout *(Lycodapus mandibularis)*; penpoint gunnel *(Apodichthys flavidus)*; petrale sole *(Eopsetta jordani)*; pile perch *(Rhacochilus vacca)*; pink salmon *(Oncorhynchus gorbuscha)*; pinpoint lampfish *(Nannobrachium regale)*; plainfin midshipman *(Porichthys notatus)*; pricklebreast poacher *(Stellerina*

xyosterna); prickly sculpin *(Cottus asper)*; prowfish *(Zaprora silenus)*; Puget Sound rockfish *(Sebastes emphaeus)*; Puget Sound sculpin *(Ruscarius meanyi)*; pygmy poacher *(Odontopyxis trispinosa)*; pygmy snailfish *(Lipariscus nanus)* • queenfish *(Seriphus politus)*; quillback rockfish *(Sebastes maliger)*; quillfish *(Ptilichthys goodei)* • ragfish *(Icosteus aenigmaticus)*; red brotula *(Brosmophycis marginata)*; red gunnel *(Pholis schultzi)*; red Irish lord *(Hemilepidotus hemilepidotus)*; redbanded rockfish *(Sebastes babcocki)*; redstripe rockfish *(Sebastes proriger)*; rex sole *(Glyptocephalus zachirus)*; ribbed sculpin *(Triglops pingelii)*; ribbon prickleback *(Phytichthys chirus)*; ribbon snailfish *(Liparis cyclopus)*; ringtail snailfish *(Liparis rutteri)*; rock greenling *(Hexagrammos lagocephalus)*; rock prickleback *(Xiphister mucosus)*; rockhead *(Bothragonus swanii)*; rockweed gunnel *(Apodichthys fucorum)*; rosethorn rockfish *(Sebastes helvomaculatus)*; rosy rockfish *(Sebastes rosaceus)*; rosylip sculpin *(Ascelichthys rhodorus)*; roughback sculpin *(Chitonotus pugetensis)*; rougheye rockfish *(Sebastes aleutianus)*; roughspine sculpin *(Triglops macellus)* • sablefish *(Anoplopoma fimbria)*; saddleback gunnel *(Pholis ornata)*; saddleback sculpin *(Oligocottus rimensis)*; sailfin sculpin *(Nautichthys oculofasciatus)*; salmon shark *(Lamna ditropis)*; sand sole *(Psettichthys melanostictus)*; sandpaper skate *(Bathyraja kincaidii)*; scalyhead sculpin *(Artedius harringtoni)*; sharpchin rockfish *(Sebastes zacentrus)*; sharpnose sculpin *(Clinocottus acuticeps)*;

sheepshead minnow *(Cyprinodon variegatus)*; shiner perch *(Cymatogaster aggregata)*; shortfin eelpout *(Lycodes brevipes)*; shortspine thornyhead *(Sebastolobus alascanus)*; showy snailfish *(Liparis pulchellus)*; silver surfperch *(Hyperprosopon ellipticum)*; silvergray rockfish *(Sebastes brevispinis)*; silverspotted sculpin *(Blepsias cirrhosus)*; slender cockscomb *(Anoplarchus insignis)*; slender snipe eel *(Nemichthys scolopaceus)*; slender sole *(Lyopsetta exilis)*; slim sculpin *(Radulinus asprellus)*; slimy snailfish *(Liparis mucosus)*; slipskin snailfish *(Liparis fucensis)*; smallhead eelpout *(Lycodapus parviceps)*; smooth alligatorfish *(Anoplagonus inermis)*; smootheye poacher *(Xeneretmus leiops)*; smoothhead sculpin *(Artedius lateralis)*; snake prickleback *(Lumpenus sagitta)*; sockeye salmon *(Oncorhynchus nerka)*; soft sculpin *(Psychrolutes sigalutes)*; southern rock sole *(Lepidopsetta bilineata)*; speckled sanddab *(Citharichthys stigmaeus)*; spinycheek starsnout *(Bathyagonus infraspinatus)*; spinyhead sculpin *(Dasycottus setiger)*; spinynose sculpin *(Asemichthys taylori)*; splitnose rockfish *(Sebastes diploproa)*; spotfin sculpin *(Icelinus tenuis)*; spotted ratfish *(Hydrolagus colliei)*; spotted snailfish *(Liparis callyodon)*; spotted spiny dogfish *(Squalus suckleyi)*; starry flounder *(Platichthys stellatus)*; steelhead *(Oncorhynchus mykiss)*; striped bass *(Morone saxatilis)*; striped seaperch *(Embiotoca lateralis)*; stripetail rockfish *(Sebastes saxicola)*; sturgeon poacher *(Podothecus accipenserinus)*; surf smelt *(Hypomesus pretiosus)* • tadpole sculpin *(Psychrolutes paradoxus)*; tadpole snailfish *(Nectoliparis pelagicus)*; thornback sculpin *(Paricelinus hopliticus)*; threadfin sculpin *(Icelinus filamentosus)*; threespine stickleback *(Gasterosteus aculeatus)*; thresher shark *(Alopias vulpinus)*; tidepool sculpin *(Oligocottus maculosus)*; tidepool snailfish *(Liparis florae)*; tiger rockfish *(Sebastes nigrocinctus)*; tubenose poacher *(Pallasina barbata)*; tubesnout *(Aulorhynchus flavidus)* • vermilion rockfish *(Sebastes miniatus)* • walleye pollock *(Gadus chalcogrammus)*; warty poacher *(Chesnonia verrucosa)*; wattled eelpout *(Lycodes palearis)*; western river lamprey *(Lampetra ayresii)*; white barracudina *(Arctozenus risso)*; white croaker *(Genyonemus lineatus)*; white seabass *(Atractoscion nobilis)*; white seaperch *(Phanerodon furcatus)*; white sturgeon *(Acipenser transmontanus)*; whitebait smelt *(Allosmerus elongatus)*; whitebarred prickleback *(Poroclinus rothrocki)*; whitespotted greenling *(Hexagrammos stelleri)*; widow rockfish *(Sebastes entomelas)*; wolf eel *(Anarrhichthys ocellatus)* • y-prickleback *(Lumpenopsis hypochroma)*; yelloweye rockfish *(Sebastes ruberrimus)*; yellowfin sole *(Limanda aspera)*; yellowtail rockfish *(Sebastes flavidus)*

BIRDS OF THE SALISH SEA

American avocet *(Recurvirostra americana)*; American bittern *(Botaurus lentiginosus)*; American coot *(Fulica americana)*; American golden plover *(Pluvialis dominica)*; American goldfinch *(Spinus tristis)*; American white pelican *(Pelecanus erythrorynchos)*; American wigeon *(Anas americana)*; ancient murrelet *(Synthliboramphus antiquus)*; arctic loon *(Gavia arctica)*; arctic tern *(Sterna paradisaea)* • Baird's sandpiper *(Calidris bairdii)*; bald eagle *(Haliaeetus leucocephalus)*; band-tailed pigeon *(Patagioenas fasciata)*; bar-tailed godwit *(Limosa lapponica)*; Barrow's goldeneye *(Bucephala islandica)*; belted kingfisher *(Megaceryle alcyon)*; black-bellied plover *(Pluvialis squatarola)*; black oystercatcher *(Haematopus bachmani)*; black scoter *(Melanitta nigra)*; black tern *(Chlidonias niger)*; black turnstone *(Arenaria melanocephala)*; black-footed albatross *(Phoebastria nigripes)*; black-headed gull *(Chroicocephalus ridibundus)*; black-legged kittiwake *(Rissa tridactyla)*; black-necked stilt *(Himantopus mexicanus)*; blue-winged teal *(Anas discors)*; Bonaparte's gull *(Chroicocephalus philadelphia)*; Brandt's cormorant *(Phalacrocorax penicillatus)*; brant *(Branta bernicula)*; brown pelican *(Pelecanus occidentalis)*; buff-breasted sandpiper *(Tryngites subruficollis)*; bufflehead *(Bucephala albeola)*; Buller's shearwater *(Puffinus bulleri)* • cackling goose *(Branta hutchinsii)*; California gull *(Larus californicus)*; Canada goose *(Branta canadensis)*; canvasback *(Aythya valisineria)*; Caspian tern *(Sterna caspia)*; Cassin's auklet *(Ptychoramphus aleuticus)*; cattle egret *(Bubulcus ibis)*; cinnamon teal *(Anas*

cyanoptera); Clark's grebe *(Aechmophorus clarkii)*; common crow *(Corvus brachyrhynchos)*; common goldeneye *(Bucephala clangula)*; common loon *(Gavia immer)*; common merganser *(Mergus merganser)*; common murre *(Uria aalge)*; common raven *(Corvus corax)*; common tern *(Sterna hirundo)* • double-crested cormorant *(Phalacrocorax auritus)*; dunlin *(Calidris alpina)* • eared grebe *(Podiceps nigricollis)*; emperor goose *(Chen canagica)*; Eurasian wigeon *(Anas penelope)* • flesh-footed shearwater *(Puffinus carneipes)*; fork-tailed storm-petrel *(Oceanodroma furcata)*; Forster's tern *(Sterna forsteri)*; Franklin's gull *(Leucophaeus pipixcan)* • gadwall *(Anas strepera)*; glaucous gull *(Larus hyperboreus)*; glaucous-winged gull *(Larus glaucescens)*; golden-crowned sparrow *(Zonotrichia atricapilla)*; great blue heron *(Ardea herodias)*; great egret *(Ardea alba)*; great horned owl *(Bubo virginianus)*; greater scaup *(Aythya marila)*; greater white-fronted goose *(Anser albifrons)*; greater yellowlegs *(Tringa melanoleuca)*; green heron *(Butorides virescens)*; green-winged teal *(Anas crecca)*; gyrfalcon *(Falco rusticolus)* • harlequin duck *(Histrionicus histrionicus)*; Heermann's gull *(Larus heermanni)*; herring gull *(Larus argentatus)*; hooded merganser *(Lophodytes cucullatus)*; horned grebe *(Podiceps auritus)*; horned puffin *(Fratercula corniculata)*; Hudsonian godwit *(Limosa haemastica)* • Iceland gull *(Larus glaucoides)* • killdeer *(Charadrius vociferous)*; king eider *(Somateria spectabilis)* • lapland longspur *(Calcarius lapponicus)*;

Leach's storm-petrel *(Oceanodroma leucorhoa)*; least sandpiper *(Calidris minutilla*; lesser scaup *(Aythya affinis)*; lesser yellowlegs *(Tringa flavipes)*; little gull *(Hydrocoloeus minutus)*; long-billed curlew *(Numenius americanus)*; long-billed dowitcher *(Limnodromus scolopaceus)*; long-billed murrelet *(Brachyramphus perdix)*; long-tailed duck *(Clangula hyemalis)*; long-tailed jaeger *(Stercorarius longicaudus)* • mallard *(Anas platyrhynchos)*; marbled godwit *(Limosa fedoa)*; marbled murrelet *(Brachyramphus marmoratus)*; marsh wren *(Cistothorus palustris)*; merlin *(Falco columbarius)*; mew gull *(Larus canus)*; mute swan *(Cygnus olor)* • northern fulmar *(Fulmarus glacialis)*; northern harrier *(Circus cyaneus)*; northern pintail *(Anas acuta)*; northern shoveler *(Anas clypeata)*; northwestern crow *(Corvus caurinus)* • osprey *(Pandion haliaetus)* • Pacific golden plover *(Pluvialis fulva)*; Pacific loon *(Gavia pacifica)*; parasitic jaeger *(Stercorarius parasiticus)*; pectoral sandpiper *(Calidris melanotos)*; pelagic cormorant *(Phalacrocorax pelagicus)*; peregrine falcon *(Falco peregrinus)*; pied-billed grebe *(Podilymbus podiceps)*; pigeon guillemot *(Cepphus columba)*; pink-footed shearwater *(Puffinus creatopus)*; pomarine jaeger *(Stercorarius pomarinus)*; purple martin *(Progne subis)* • red knot *(Calidris canutus)*; red phalarope *(Phalaropus fulicaria)*; red-breasted merganser *(Mergus serrator)*; red-necked grebe *(Podiceps grisegena)*; red-necked

phalarope *(Phalaropus lobatus)*; red-tailed hawk *(Buteo jamaicensis)*; red-throated loon *(Gavia stellata)*; redhead *(Aythya americana)*; rhinoceros auklet *(Cerorhinca monocerata)*; ring-billed gull *(Larus delawarensis)*; ring-necked duck *(Aythya collaris)*; rock sandpiper *(Calidris ptilocnemis)*; Ross' goose *(Chen rossii)*; rough-legged hawk *(Buteo lagopus)*; ruddy duck *(Oxyura jamaicensis)*; ruddy turnstone *(Arenaria interpres)*; ruff *(Philomachus pugnax)* • Sabine's gull *(Xema sabini)*; sanderling *(Calidris alba)*; sandhill crane *(Grus canadensis)*; savannah sparrow *(Passerculus sandwichensis)*; semipalmated plover *(Charadrius semipalmatus)*; semipalmated sandpiper *(Caldris pusilla)*; sharp-tailed sandpiper *(Calidris acuminata)*; short-billed dowitcher *(Limnodromus griseus)*; short-eared owl *(Asio flammeus)*; short-tailed shearwater *(Puffinus tenuirostris)*; slaty-backed gull *(Larus schistisagus)*; snow bunting *(Plectrophenax nivalis)*; snow goose *(Chen caerulescens)*; snowy owl *(Bubo scandiacus)*; sooty shearwater *(Puffinus griseus)*; sora *(Porzana carolina)*; south polar skua *(Stercorarius maccormicki)*; spotted sandpiper *(Actitis macularius)*; stilt sandpiper *(Calidris himantopus)*; surf scoter *(Melanitta perspicillata)*; surfbird *(Aphriza virgata)* • Thayer's gull *(Larus thayeri)*; trumpeter swan *(Cygnus buccinator)*; tufted duck *(Aythya fuligula)*; tufted puffin *(Fatercula cirrhata)*; tundra swan *(Cygnus columbianus)*; turkey vulture *(Cathartes aura)* • Virginia rail *(Rallus limicola)* • wandering tattler *(Tringa incana)*; western grebe *(Aechmophorus occidentalis)*; western gull *(Larus occidentalis)*; western sandpiper *(Calidris mauri)*; whimbrel *(Numenius phaeopus)*; white-crowned sparrow *(Zonotrichia leucophrys)*; white-winged scoter *(Melanitta fusca)*; willet *(Tringa semipalmata)*; Wilson's phalarope *(Phalaropus tricolor)*; Wilson's snipe *(Gallinago delicata)* • yellow-billed loon *(Gavia adamsii)*

MAMMALS OF THE SALISH SEA

Baird's beaked whale *(Berardius bairdii)*; beaver *(Castor canadensis)*; black bear *(Ursus americanus)*; bottlenose dolphin *(Tursiops truncatus)*; Bryde's whale *(Balaenoptera edeni)* • California sea lion *(Zalophus californianus)*; Columbian black-tailed

deer *(Odocoileus hemionus columbianus)*; Cuvier's beaked whale *(Ziphius cavirostris)* • Dall's porpoise *(Phocoenoides dalli)* • false killer whale *(Pseudorca crassidens)*; fin whale *(Balaenoptera physalis)* • gray whale *(Eschrichtius robustus)*; grizzly bear *(Ursus arctos)* • harbor porpoise *(Phocoena phocoena)*; harbor seal *(Phoca vitulina)*; Hubb's beaked whale *(Mesoplodon carlhubbsi)*; humpback whale *(Megaptera novaengliae)* • killer whale *(Orcinus orca)* • long-beaked common dolphin *(Delphinus capensis)* • mink *(Neovison vison)*; minke whale *(Balaenoptera acutorostrata)*; muskrat *(Odatra zibethicus)* • North American river otter *(Lontra canadensis)*; northern elephant seal *(Mirounga angustirostris)*; northern fur seal *(Callorhinus ursinus)*; northern right whale dolphin *(Lissodelphis borealis)* • Pacific white-sided dolphin *(Lagenorhynchus obliquidens)*; pygmy sperm whale *(Kogia brevirostris)* • raccoon *(Procyon lotor)*; red fox *(Vulpes vulpes)*; ribbon seal *(Histriophoca fasciata)*; Risso's dolphin *(Grampus griseus)* • sea otter *(Enyhydra lutris)*; short-beaked common dolphin *(Delphinus delphis)*; short-finned pilot whale *(Globicephala macrorhynchus)*; Stejneger's beaked whale *(Mesoplodon stejnegeri)*; Steller sea lion *(Eumetopias jubatus)*; striped dolphin *(Stenella coeruleoalba)*

FURTHER READING

Allen, S. G., J. Mortenson, S. Webb. *Field Guide to Marine Mammals of the Pacific Coast: Baja, California, Oregon, Washington, British Columbia*. Berkeley: University of California, 2011.

Angell, T., and K. C. Balcomb III. *Marine Birds and Mammals of Puget Sound*. Seattle: Puget Sound, 1982.

Blanchard, Rebecca, and Nancy Davenport, eds. *Contemporary Coast Salish Art*. Seattle: Stonington Gallery and University of Washington Press, 2005.

Dietrich, William. *Natural Grace: The Charm, Wonder & Lessons of Pacific Northwest Animals & Plants*. Seattle: University of Washington Press, 2003.

Easterbrook, Don J. *A Walk Through Geologic Time from Mt. Baker to Bellingham Bay*. Bellingham: Chuckanut Editions, 2010.

Glavin, T. *The Last Great Sea: A Voyage Through the Human and Natural History of the North Pacific Ocean*. Vancouver: Greystone, 2000.

Gough, B. *Juan de Fuca's Strait: Voyages in the Waterway of Forgotten Dreams*. Madeira Park, B.C.: Harbour, 2012.

Hall, D. *Beneath Cold Seas: The Underwater Wilderness of the Pacific Northwest*. Seattle: University of Washington Press, 2011.

Harbo, R. M. *Whelks to Whales: Coastal Marine Life of the Pacific Northwest*. Madeira Park, B.C.: Harbour, 2011.

Harrington, Sheila, and Judi Stevenson, eds. *Islands in the Salish Sea: A Community Atlas*. Surrey, B.C.: TouchWood Editions, 2007.

Heffernan, Trova. *Where the Salmon Run: The Life and Legacy of Billy Frank Jr.* Seattle: University of Washington Press and the Washington State Heritage Center, 2012.

Helvarg, D. *50 Ways to Save the Ocean*. Maui, Hawaii: Inner Ocean, 2006.

Jensen, G. C. *Crabs and Shrimps of the Pacific Coast: A Guide to Shallow-Water Decapods from Southeastern Alaska to the Mexican Border*. Bremerton, Wash.: MolaMarine, 2014.

Kozloff, E. N. *Marine Invertebrates of the Pacific Northwest*. Seattle: University of Washington Press, 1996.

Kruckeberg, A. R. *The Natural History of Puget Sound Country*. Seattle: University of Washington Press, 1991.

Lamb, A., and P. Edgell. *Coastal Fishes of the Pacific Northwest*. Madeira Park, B.C.: Harbour, 1986.

Lamb, A., and B. P. Hanby. *Marine Life of the Pacific Northwest: A Photographic Encyclopedia of Invertebrates, Seaweeds and Selected Fishes*. Madeira Park, B.C.: Harbour, 2005.

Layzer, J. A., ed. *Natural Experiments: Ecosystem-Based Management and the Environment*. Cambridge: MIT, 2008.

Lichen, Patricia K. *Brittle Stars & Mudbugs: An Uncommon Field Guide to Northwest Shorelines & Wetlands*. Seattle: Sasquatch Books, 2001.

Lombard, J. *Saving Puget Sound: A Conservation Strategy for the 21st Century*. Bethesda: American Fisheries Society, 2006.

Love, M. S. *Certainly More Than You Want to Know About the Fishes of the Pacific Coast*. Santa Barbara: Really Big Press, 2011.

Love, M. S., M. Yoklavich, and L. Thorsteinson. *The Rockfishes of the Northeast Pacific*. Berkeley: University of California Press, 2002.

Ludvigsen, R., and Graham Beard. *West Coast Fossils: A Guide to the Ancient Life of Vancouver Island*. Madeira Park, B.C.: Harbour, 1997.

Mapes, Lynda V. *Elwha: A River Reborn*. Seattle: Mountaineers Books, 2013.

Norse, E. A. *Ancient Forests of the Pacific Northwest*. Washington, D.C.: Island Press, 1990.

Osborne, R., J. Calambokidis, and E. M. Dorsey. *A Guide to Marine Mammals of Greater Puget Sound*. Edited by D. Haley. Anacortes: Island Publishers, 1998.

Ruckelshaus, M. H., and M. M. McClure. Sound Science: Synthesizing Ecological and Socioeconomic Information about the Puget Sound Ecosystem. U.S. Dept. of Commerce, National Oceanic & Atmospheric Administration (NMFS), Northwest Fisheries Science Center; prepared in cooperation with the Sound Science collaborative team, Seattle, 2007.

Ruth, Maria Mudd. *Rare Bird: Pursuing the Mystery of the Marbled Murrelet*. Seattle: Mountaineers Books, 2013.

Safina, C. *Song for the Blue Ocean*. New York: Holt, 1998.

Stein, Julie K. *Exploring Coast Salish Prehistory: The Archaeology of San Juan Island*. Seattle: University of Washington Press, 2000.

Stewart, Hilary. *Cedar*. Seattle: University of Washington Press, 1995.

Suttles, Wayne. *Coast Salish Essays*. Vancouver: Talonbooks, 1987.

Touchie, Rodger D. *Edward S. Curtis: Above the Medicine Line*. Vancouver: Heritage House, 2010.

Vernon, Susan. *Rainshadow World: A Naturalist's Year in the San Juan Islands*. Friday Harbor, Wash.: Archipelago Press, 2010.

Wadewitz, L. K. *The Nature of Borders: Salmon, Boundaries, and Bandits in the Salish Sea*. Seattle: University of Washington Press, 2012.

Wahl, T. R., B. Tweit, and S. G. Mlodinow. *Birds of Washington: Status and Distribution*. Corvallis: Oregon State University Press, 2005.

Wallace, S., and B. Gisborne. *Basking Sharks: The Slaughter of BC's Gentle Giants*. Vancouver: New Star, 2006.

Yates, S. *Marine Wildlife: From Puget Sound Through the Inside Passage*. Seattle: Sasquatch, 1998.

Yates, S. *Orcas, Eagles, & Kings: Puget Sound & Georgia Strait*. Boca Raton, Fla.: Primavera, 1992.

Acknowledgments

Our inspiration for this book arrived on an ocean swell—a reminder that a celebration of the Salish Sea's biodiversity and enduring beauty was long overdue. The often-quoted adage "it takes a village to raise a child" applies equally well to the daunting challenge of producing a book about a region as geologically and biologically complex as the Salish Sea. It would not have been possible without the creative vision and skill, scientific expertise, and encouragement of many people. The collaborative skills and expertise of our two conservation-focused nonprofits, Cloud Ridge Naturalists and the SeaDoc Society, made it possible for us to create a book that reveals the essential magic of the Salish Sea in a way that we hope will inspire the next generation of conservation stewards.

Audrey's profound gratitude goes to her late husband and mentor, Jim Benedict, who showed her over the course of his 45 years of multidisciplinary research that getting the science "right" and expressing the beauty of a place are never incompatible in teaching or in writing; it is the best legacy we can leave for future generations. When it comes to friends and family, she's always been honored by their loving support and belief in her. Even her Labrador retriever, Scruggs, forgives the vagaries of a writer's life as long as the desk light goes off eventually.

Joseph K. Gaydos would like to thank his family and friends for their patience, their understanding, and their encouragement while he wrote and was immersed in yet another scientific paper about the marvelous creatures and workings of the Salish Sea. As he says, his family and friends are his backbone and nothing would be possible without that loving support.

We also extend our heartfelt thanks to SeaDoc's Director Kirsten Gilardi, the Orcas Island–based staff, especially Jean Lyle and Joe Thoron, SeaDoc Society board members, and the many supporters who believe in the organization's mission and work in the Salish Sea.

Grateful acknowledgments to the following people for providing scientific information, consultation, and key concepts for inclusion in this book: K. Andrews, K. Balcom, L. Barrett-Lennard, R. Barsh, M. Ben-David, A. Burger, J. Calambokidis, T. Carpenter, D. Costa, G. Davis, R. DeLong, M. Dethier, D. Ellifrit, C. Emmons, J. K. B. Ford, B. Frank, F. Graner, G. Greene, J. Hahn, G. Hammerson, M. Haulena, M. Holt, G. Hood, S. Jeffries, G. C. Jensen, C. K. Johnson, T. Klinger, M. Kongsgaard, J. Konovsky, L. Lahner, S. Larsen, C. Mills, M. Murphy, K. Naish, J. Newton, D. Noren, D. Nysewander, W. Palsson, S. Pearson, T. Peitsch, K. Rawson, P. Ross, Seattle Aquarium staff, J. Smith, J. Stein, A. Summers, T. Tinker, B. Vadopalas, Vancouver Aquarium staff, B. Webber, K. Wellman, and B. Wright.

We would also like to extend our thanks to Gary Luke and his staff at Sasquatch Books for their enthusiastic embrace of a book on the Salish Sea and for their facilitation and unwavering support during all phases of the project.

CLOUD RIDGE PUBLISHING

We extend our profound thanks to Cloud Ridge Publishing's extraordinary book production team—seasoned professionals and a dream team in every sense of the word. The multifaceted expertise, skill, creative energy, commitment to excellence, and patience they bring to everything they do is remarkable beyond measure. Every page in this book reflects their consummate artistry and skill.

Publisher: Audrey D. Benedict

Project manager and photo editor: Wendy Shattil

Photo editor: Bob Rozinski

Book designer: Ann W. Douden

Editor: Alice Levine

Production coordinator: Betsy Armstrong

Proofreader: Faith Marcovecchio

Our Donors

Without the generous financial support and underwriting of The Benedict Family Foundation and the matching gifts by SeaDoc Society supporters, this book would not have been possible.

We would like to extend our gratitude to The Anders Foundation, Richard and Dawn Bangert, Sidney Brinckerhoff, Betty Corbett, Kevin and Mary Daniels, Leslie Dierauf and Jim Hurley, Jim and Laura Donald, Stacy Farnsworth, Frank Greer and Stephanie Solien, Wally and Susan Gudgell, H. S. Wright III and Kate Janeway, Martha Kongsgaard and Peter Goldman, Alice and Judah Levine, Pacific Catalyst: Bill and Shannon Bailey, Ingrid Rasch, Stu and Lee Rolfe, Jeff and Kim Seely, Craig Tall, and Tulalip Tribes.

PHOTO CREDITS

The extraordinary images in this book transport the reader on a voyage of discovery that words alone could never achieve. We extend our heartfelt gratitude and admiration to the professional and amateur photographers whose images were chosen for this book. Their photographs reveal a profound sense of place and present the intricate beauty of the Salish Sea in a way that will inspire the next generation of conservation stewards.

Steph Abegg 24, 32, 130

Ken Archer iii, 55 (top), 86, 87 (top left, top right), 89 (top), 94

Robin W. Baird/Cascadian Research Collective 113 (top)

Glenn Bartley 42 (bottom), 49 (bottom left), 100, 101 (bottom left), 108 (top)

Brett Baunton 37

Les Bazco/*Vancouver Sun* 118

Audrey Benedict 20 (bottom left, right), 99 (top)

Bill Benedict 17 (left)

Photo by Byrne, Whatcom Museum #1975.103.106, Bellingham, WA 133

Marc Chamberlain v (second from bottom), 3 (left), 30, 31, 54, 56 (bottom left, top middle, top right, center middle, center right, bottom right), 62 (left), 70 (all), 73 (top left, bottom left), 75 (inset), 77, 83 (top), 126 (bottom), 137 (right), 139, 140 (right), 144, 148

Paul Colangelo ix (bottom), 21, 23, 47 (left), 49 (top right), 52, 59, 131, 132

Brandon Cole v (top), vi, vii (top, second from bottom), viii, 1 (inset), 5, 33 (top), 46, 47 (right), 55 (bottom), 56 (top left), 57 (top left), 63 (left), 68, 69 (top), 71 (inset, bottom), 72 (all), 73 (top right, bottom right), 74, 78–79, 79 (inset, bottom), 80–81, 82, 109, 110, 111, 122, 123 (left), 125

Drew Collins vii (second from top), 64, 69 (bottom), back cover

Edward S. Curtis, Charles Deering McCormick Library of Special Collections, Northwestern University Library 4, 119 (bottom)

Manual Rod del Pozo 124 (all)

John D'Onofrio v (second from top), 13 (left), 14, 18

Florian Graner ix (second from bottom), 7 (right), 60, 63 (right), 71 (top), 80 (inset), 120, 126 (top)

Phil Green 3 (right), 57 (bottom left), 58 (all), 76 (bottom)

Amy Gulick 140 (left)

Geoff Hammerson 53 (right), 98, 99 (bottom), 103, 142 (left)

Brad Hill ix (top), 96, 97

Jared Hobbs 45

Mark Hobson 48

W. G. Hood 52 (inset)

Garth Lenz 38, 40

Chris Linder 136

Robin Lindsey front cover (bottom), i, 10

John Lowman 3 (center), 8, 26, 85, 91 (top), 102, 134 (bottom), 138, 142 (right)

James Maya 112, 114, 128

NASA Earth Observatory 34

National Oceanic and Atmospheric Administration/ Department of Commerce, Mandy Lindeberg, NOAA/NMFS/AKFSC 78 (left)

Pete Naylor 73 (center right), 83 (bottom)

Kathleen Newell/U.W. School of Oceanography 65, 66–67

Jessica Newley ix (second from top), 33 (bottom), 76 (top), 107, 135

Janna Nichols 61

Roberta Olenick 88

James R. Page 134 (inset)

Jim Ramaglia 81 (right)

Lee Rentz 42 (top left)

Tom Roorda 35

Kevin Schafer front cover (top), xii, 15, 62 (right)

Neil Schulman xi, 11, 123 (right)

John Scurlock 22

Wendy Shattil/Bob Rozinski 6, 12, 13 (right), 17 (right), 50, 90, 93, 121

Alan Sirulnikoff 28

Connor Stefanison v (bottom), 41 (bottom), 42 (top right), 43 (right), 84

Taylor Shellfish Farms 127 (all)

Jared Towers 95, 104, 108 (bottom left, bottom right)

Gerrit Vyn 89 (bottom)

Traci Walter 106, 137 (left), 145 (right)

Craig Weakley vii (bottom), 57 (top right), 92

Ethan Welty 20 (top left), 41 (top), 53 (left), 116–117, 119 (top)

Ethan Welty/Aurora Photos 129

Monika Wieland 113 (bottom)

Art Wolfe iv, 2, 16, 19, 36, 39, 51 (inset), 87 (bottom), 91 (bottom), 115

Tim Zurowski 44, 49 (middle left), 57 (bottom right), 101 (top left, bottom right), 141, 146

Ocean gardens occur on the threshold of the deeper sea, where bull kelp can grow as tall as a tree and animals "bloom" like flowers.